LAWS OF INFLUENCE

7even Lessons in Transformational Leadership

CHARLES MWEWA

ACP
PRESS

DEDICATION

To the memory of my father,
ZACHARIAH KALUBEYA MWEWA

CONTENTS

FOREWORD

Charles Mwewa has written this inspirational and motivating book which is a "must read" for everyone from all walks of life. His ideas are holistic and well-rounded as he discusses the "Laws of Influence." He has captured vividly leadership and other principles which he elaborates and makes situational for his readers. This is a non-traditional approach, and one that can be attributed to the positive feedback from across three continents – North America, Europe and Africa.

The author who in real-life is called a leader, shares personal experiences, introduces well-named personalities and their stories to illustrate the defined principles. Charles Mwewa has, indeed, given us not a book but a document to which we will return and re-read as it provokes the reader to act and embrace the ideas presented. A truly inspirational writer and a great motivational book thereby a recipe for good reading, awareness and learning. It makes you believe you can, and actually provides the tools for influence.

Hon. Jean Augustine, P.C.
Ontario's Fairness Commissioner
(Former Deputy Speaker of Canada)

INTRODUCTION

This book is not on the theory of influence. It is not a textbook of social psychology, either. This book is about the author pouring his heart into the reader's. It is about attested principles and tested laws that are proven to work time and again. Influencing people and winning them to your side is not as difficult as most people think. In this book you will learn how to gain the confidence of almost any person, how to win friends, and have an impact on society. This book is for everyone, and, in particular, two kinds of people will appreciate it. The first are those who desire to leave a mark on time by molding contemporaries, and exerting an influence which stretches far into the future. And the second are those who are leaders.

A man's life is as important as the impact it has on others. We remember people who have selflessly given of themselves for the benefit of others; but we least award accolades to those who live for themselves. We celebrate men and women who have considered their own lives of less value than that which they have done for others. And it is these people who truly influence their world.

This book has been organized according to the following plan. There are seven parts each consisting of a chapter or chapters. Each part supplies the opportunity to describe one of the seven laws of influence. Fundamental materials about each law of influence are presented in subheadings, which should assist in understanding the discussions contained in each chapter.

The power to influence lies partly in contribution. The best kind of contribution is when you sincerely and tirelessly help others to win and succeed in life. You are a true champion, and a winner, when you set a good example and help another human being to win. Helping others, whether they are members of your immediate family, neighbors, relatives, a nation or total strangers, is the best way of contributing to life. This aspect of influence is dealt with in Part One of this book.

One group of people who have the opportunity to have an impact on people are leaders. But it is not every kind of leader who influences people for the better.

Effective leaders are those who bring out the best in people by stimulating them to achieve that which is impossible. They are transformational leaders. One way in which they do this is by genuinely becoming interested in people and by building relationships. They achieve this through persuasion.

Persuasion takes several faces. To some, persuasion is simply convincing your boss that you deserve a pay raise. It could also be through inspiration, such as cajoling a team to finish a project or getting your partner to see your point of view. To the larger extent, every form of influence involves persuasion. Persuasion is mostly done by expanding your sphere of influence. This mainly involves persuading other people to be your champions, so that, in turn, they will be able to connect you to areas you would otherwise not have had access.

Such kind of persuasive influence is short-lived and of less concern in this book. The type of persuasion emphasized here is a kind aimed at positively affecting people's lives. People have used their influence to coerce and manipulate others. And sometimes they have succeeded in getting things done for them. But that is not truly influencing people. That is, to put it matter of factly, forcing people to do what they want, against the people's own will. The goal of persuasion is to influence the subject to make decisions that are reasonable. It is not merely informing or enlightening people; it is persuading them to turn from bad to good, from living a meaningless life to living a life of purpose.

Persuasion is designed to change people's attitudes. Attitudes are born out of behavioral tendencies which have come to shape one's view of life and other people. When one's attitude towards another person or thing is good, his or her approach and actions will be good as well. To change a person or people, one has to change his or her attitudes first. This book has dealt with this aspect of influence in details in Part Two.

Real influencing is, however, far subtler and fairer than simply persuasion. For one thing, it requires good interpersonal and communication skills. For another, it entails the ability to get people to want to support, vote for, purchase, or change behavior. When you use your influencing skills well, people will naturally like to be with and around you. You will be sought after like a rare commodity. There is a kind of exciting buzz, or sense that things happen when you are around. When you are a true influencer, you will not only persuade people with words, but you will also have an impact on them by the way you care for them.

The essence of caring lies in the fact that everyone, regardless of race, background, age, gender, nationality, skin color, education, status in life, sexual orientation, etcetera, is important and deserving of your attention and care. That is when you begin to live life to the fullest. When you discriminate and draw boundaries of apartheid, racism, bigotry, prejudice, intolerance, bias, or chauvinism, you are incapable of being a true human leader. Caring is a basic human instinct and the flame that keeps human life alive. This aspect of influencing people is covered extensively in Part Three.

Influencing people is analogous with seedtime and harvest time. According to the Law of Seedtime, what you sow is what you will also reap. How you live your life, and the impact you leave behind you, depend, to the larger extent, on the Law of Seedtime. The *Law of Harvest* postulates that you reap more than what you sow. The Law of Seedtime implies reaping in quality, but the Law of Harvest entails reaping in quantity. And Part Four deals with this aspect of influence at length

In life, the way you finish is more important than the way you began. This means that you must strive to run your race with integrity. It also means that you should treat people on your path the way you would like them to treat you. Unless you are pretty sure you will never come down, the way you relate to the people on your way up is very important. You might meet the same people on your way down. Influencing people in this regard means giving your best for them and sacrificing your best for their glory. It is not just leading people if you are a leader—it is leading them with concern and love. And this is the subject of discussion in Part Five.

The simplest formula for influencing people is to attract them to you. It has been said that there is no leadership without followership. A good leader is the one who attracts people to his or her side. The power to retain the kind of people who will enable you to fulfill a particular goal or task is a skill every leader must learn. There are a few basic things, however, which leaders must do to attract people, and these, including the Law of Attraction, have been intensely discussed in Part Six.

The difference between leaders and followers is in the way they view the future. Leaders envision a future filled with possibilities, while followers live for the moment. Your job as a leader is to influence your workers, subordinates, followers, or a nation, to see the future the way it must be. It is to help them dream beyond their present limitations and fears. When they achieve these lofty dreams, they will bring you to the fore. People rarely forget those who helped them to dream and who inspired them to pursue those dreams to their successful ends. In Part Seven, this aspect of influence is examined in substantial details.

The *Laws of Influence* is not a work of genius; it is not a great work of accomplishment, either. This book may not even make the list of the world's bestseller. That is not the reason I wrote it. However, remember, if at your death-bed you did all except what is written about in this book, your name will die with you. If you will do even just half of what is discussed in this book, to me and to those you love, you are a hero.

This book was first published as *The Seven Laws of Influence* by a US publisher in 2007. Without altering content but only updating it where required, the same book is now titled, *Laws of Influence: Seven lessons in transformational leadership*.

Charles Mwewa
Ottawa, Canada
2021

PART I

THE LAW OF CONTRIBUTION

1

LIVING FOR A LARGER CAUSE

*Through contribution, we leave marks
that will inspire others to see the light in
the dark of life's night.*
— Charles Mwewa

On July 11th, 2007, a man known as *Mr. Toronto,* died at the age of 92. Ed Mirvish was a Toronto businessman renowned both for his landmark discount store, Honest Ed's, and for his key role in revitalizing the city's theatre scene. Many prominent Torontonians described Ed as a man with an incredible strength of character and influence. The way he both lived and died made him a true man of the people. At his huge elaborate birthday parties Ed would lavish upon the city free turkeys.

It is not his picture walking side by side with Princes Diana that made this man famous and beloved—it was his heart. The great City of Toronto had lost one of the most generous, empathetic and friendly people the city had ever known. The significance of a man's life is in the impact it has on other people.

Ed Mirvish was a rich businessman. But he was also a good man who lived for others. Ed was a contributor. He lived for a larger cause than just making money. He died a happy man. You don't need to have lots of money to make an impact; all you need is a heart, a desire to live for other human beings.

Source of True Happiness

People have for centuries mulled over what truly makes one happy. Is it money, power, popularity, or fame? And you can add to the list of answers what you will; but these things in themselves don't bring lasting happiness. Money may bring temporary happiness to a poor person. Fame may momentarily cheer a determined personality. Power may briefly bring glee to an ambitious man. But what else does a rich man live for? Life is about contribution. The things we do for others and the manner in which we do them matter a lot. Through cheerfulness we build happy bridges. Through empathy we cross to the other side. But it is only through contribution that we leave marks that will inspire others to see the light in the dark of life's nights.

Living and Dying Happy

People will not remember your face or your great personal accomplishments, but they will remember the positive contributions you made to their lives or their community. The greatest investment in life is in the people. When you serve them with your position, money, or gifts, they live to appreciate you even after you are long gone. Contribution defines immortality: because what you do for yourself only dies with you. But what you do for others and the world outlives you and is immortal.

Snack Sunday Initiative

When we began our Snack Sunday initiative in downtown Toronto, I did not think it would have the impact it had on people. We basically provided fellowship to people who might be lonely or were left out of the rollercoaster of busy city life. The *World Influence Vision*, a leadership vision I founded in Toronto in 2006, engineered this initiative. Our motivation is based on pure love and the desire to contribute something to humanity.

The Snack Sunday initiative was a group effort. A few people gave of their valuable time and help in making sure that those meetings were successful. Clarice spent the evenings before Snack Sundays cooking for the people who would show up. Irene was ardent at fundraising for the event. Roland and Tanya gave of themselves in publicizing these events. And Mado was always there to serve the people. Even Joseph, at 73 years of age then, was involved in the distribution and logistics of the program.

The joy that comes with contribution is enormous. As we watched the homeless and the elderly eat and chat, it touched our hearts. There is nothing like it. In all my life of public ministry, I never felt that fulfilled. Together as a team, we all felt that we were contributing something to humanity. By giving of our time, energy, resources, and money, we spoke without words that we loved all God's people, no matter who they were or where they came from. We lived our lives for other people by contributing to their happiness.

Pain Suffered for Another is Gain Paid Forward

Every day gives you a chance to touch someone in a meaningful way. Pain suffered for another is gain paid forward. This principle revolves around the cycle of seasons: each season happens for, or as a direct result of, another. Summer brings sunshine, to bring beauty and rain. Fall (autumn) clears vegetation in readiness for winter. Winter holds the moisture to make planting and harvesting possible. Spring breaks the ground for harvest. Indeed, after every Winter in your life, there will be Spring. As long as the earth shall remain, planting and harvesting shall never cease, either.

In life there are always those who have to suffer so that others can benefit. These men and women selflessly give everything to help and save others. We may call them generous, or charity donors, good-hearted persons, helpers, contributors, givers, philanthropists, humanitarians, pioneers, or saviors, but whatever term we choose to assign to them, they all have one thing in common. They are willing to help, even when that means sacrificing their own personal comfort. If you want success in life, aim for service, and success will follow!

A certain man took a voyage to a place very few people would dare to go. With all the uncertainties of the journey, he embarked on what would become one of the greatest humanitarian expeditions of all times. He found and lived among people he hadn't known before. He learned their ways and even died among them. What is remarkable are the instructions he gave before he died: he commanded his retinue to bury his heart among these strange people who had become his everything. That man was the explorer Dr. David Livingstone—and the place they buried his heart is the Chitambo village in central Zambia.

Growing up, I heard so many tales. But one story which has stuck with me is *The Good Samaritan*, taken straight from the Holy Scriptures. In this story there are three major characters; two are associated with some religious aspects, while the other one isn't. Fear and pride prevent the two religious figures from ministering care to the wounded man. But the Samaritan not only tends the victim but also offers to pay for any expenses arising from his treatment.

What is the moral of this story? The story didactically tells us two things. Firstly, the story upsets the established *operandi* of social order. Religion is supposed to help the weak but in this case it doesn't. Secondly, the story reverses the expectation of social relations. Enemies weren't supposed to help each other, for the Jews were sworn enemies of the Samaritans— but here one does. In the first scenario, we all understand that certain professions are trained to perform certain duties. Thus, nurses and doctors are trained to deal with health issues. Paralegals and lawyers with legal issues! Policemen and women with safety and security issues. And the list goes on and on. It was therefore expected of the Levite and the priest to help a wounded man. But when they didn't, society held them accountable.

In the second scenario the unexpected happened. The Samaritan helped a Jew! In life you are not a hero when you do what is required of you. When a firefighter saves a person from an inferno he is merely fulfilling his obligation. But what happens when a common person risks his own safety to save another person? You agree with me that he becomes an instant hero.

The principle is: always do what is not expected of you to help another human being. Or if you are trained to do a certain job, go out of your way to not simply perform your duty, but with your job, go further and help make society better.

Giving is Living

Man's ultimate joy comes from helping another person succeed. You can do something about yourself and be happy, but you will only be more fulfilled when you do something for somebody else. This principle can be seen in everything that has life in it. The best example is in the love act. When a man gives of himself to his woman, he finds great pleasure and enormous satisfaction.

A woman, similarly, finds her own satisfaction in letting go of herself. What you give does leave your hands, but not your life. Giving and receiving are co-related. In the act of giving, there is also much room for receiving. The hand that extends to give is the same hand that stretches to receive. People for centuries have believed in the power of giving. They have understood the interrelationship between poverty and prosperity, lack and plenty, or decrease and increase. It is always more blessed to give than to receive.

But what does this saying mean? Does it mean that givers are better than receivers? Not really. This statement means that both the one who gives and the other who receives are blessed. The only difference is that the giver is blessed a bit more. The giver is more blessed, because, by giving, he has done well not only for himself, but also for the one to whom he has given. In giving, both the giver's and the recipient's desires are fulfilled. If there be any truer measure of a man than by what he does, it must be by what he gives—that's for sure.

Giving is a symbol of gratefulness. Traditionally, we all think that to be grateful we ought to have received something. And for sure it is not a good thing not to return a favor of appreciation. Conventional wisdom tells us to return a favor for a favor. But think about this: you give someone something, and you are the one who is grateful! Sounds weird, doesn't it? No, it shouldn't.

When you give, you are actually opening more doors for receiving. The more you give the more you will get. There is nothing magical about this principle. Human beings just like giving to causes which they believe will benefit them in return in some way. People will honor your efforts of selfless giving. They will go out of their ways to reciprocate in kind or in deed. When you give, you are giving yourself back in multiplied measures.

Giving is an Act of Righteousness

There is no religion; no order, and no establishment where this principle is not known. Giving is right. Giving is good. *Right is better than good.* Giving is an act of righteousness. In most cultures, people believe that giving is a good thing. Those who give may be considered righteous, while those who don't give may not. People believe that a generous heart is a cultured heart. And surely it is. When you give, you demonstrate the unfading beauty of your kind-heartedness. The heart that gives is the same heart that lives.

The best way to give is not to expect something back in return. When you give without expecting back, you're generous indeed. Giving with joy means giving with a sense of love—to touch lives and contribute to the well-being of humankind. Giving is a true expression of inner joy and spiritual mellowness. It is a strong witness to the truest state of humanness. Giving is the last line of humanitarian defense and a real mark of true greatness, because when you give you're asserting in very strong terms that you are for the very best of humanity and that you care. You are great because giving is an act of heroism.

"What is faith?" people ask. Faith is risk. It is a belief in the unseen. Faith is expectation. It is a confident declaration that what you expect will be. Faith taps into the future and experiences it in the present. Faith is about what you don't have or you can't see now, but you will have or see afterwards. When you have what you want, faith ends. That is why before there is faith, there must be hope.

Faith speaks words and does deeds even with limited information and assurance. Yet faith believes that the future is better than the past, and what is unseen is more real than what is experienced. When you give to others, you have strong faith. You believe that you are just a custodian of the Creator's interests. You are convinced of the blessedness of planting everlasting seeds into other people's lives. These seeds of benevolence will always sprout into the bounty of a fulfilled and satisfied feeling on your part. You are absolutely right, every time, when you give.

2

THE ART OF INSPIRATION

The difference between in*spiration and* ex*piration is in their first two letters.*
— *Charles Mwewa*

The greatest contribution leaders can make to mankind is to use their power to help and inspire others. Helping another to succeed is a noble task. Leadership is the selfless task of spending and being spent for the good of others. Helping other human beings is an impeccable undertaking. What has destroyed our society—is it not our insatiable appetite for gain? Even for very minute tasks done for someone else we want to be rewarded. *Nothing for nothing* is our motto, and materialism is our idol. We rarely give anything without expecting something in return. But wanting to help one another is a desirable quality we must all embrace and possess. When we help another human being succeed, we also succeed. When we give one step, we will receive two.

When that great Turkish hero renowned for stealth bravery and inexhaustible conquests,

Ertugrul Bey of the Kayi Tribe, took charge of his tribe on the way to dominate the Byzantines, he was reminded to give up his happiness and comfort for that of his people; to be the last to be fed; and, if possible, to die before anyone of his people did. That is leadership.

Sometimes it is appalling to see the ruthlessness of human nature. A person will keep on accumulating, even to his death, and will never live to enjoy his wealth. Deep down in our minds we feel that we are building lasting legacies. But someone else who didn't drop even a single drop of sweat will inherit and foil our toil. Where is human wisdom? Where is our sense of contribution? But when we help other people with what we have, we've invested in profitable ventures.

The difference between inspiration and expiration is in their first two letters. When you *in*spire, you are creating a new hope, a new perspective, and you are giving a new resolve to something that would have otherwise perished without you. You are inspiring confidence and a new look towards a workable solution. There is power in inspiring others to succeed. I have made it a habit to encourage people. And I have not stopped being amazed at how motivation makes a difference in people's lives. I believe that when you help another human succeed, you have succeeded successfully.

Whether it is on social-media, through e-mail or books, I have cultivated a habit of motivating people. There a reason why I send people encouragements every so often. I love to see people happy, and to contribute to that sense of happiness. When they read my articles, write-ups, sayings of the wise, principles for growth or a Scriptural hints, people are inspired to go on, to keep living. I believe it makes a difference between potential maximization and gift negligence. I hate to see people discouraged, because, when they are dispirited, they end up performing below their expected capacity.

Some have replied, saying that my mailer or write-ups helped them make the right decisions. Some have sent me notes of appreciation. One lady, after I wrote about the power of determination, was very thankful, because she was almost giving up on life. She said the message lifted her spirit and put her back into the game. It is these kinds of responses that enable me to continue inspiring men and women all over the world. Someone said that there is no more noble occupation in the world than to assist another human being—to help someone else succeed.

Stimulate to Achieve the Impossible

Effective leaders bring out the best in people, by stimulating them to achieve what they thought was impossible. One day Irene, then finance controller of *World Influence*, sent me an email about a lady she recommended and hired for employment while working as a supervisor at a greeting card company in Toronto. Here is exactly what she wrote:

Dear Charles,:

I just had to show off; I hired this girl when she had few prospects to do art. I was then supervisor at Carlton Cards. (At that time all she wanted to do was play a guitar and be cool—but I saw true talent when I reviewed her art portfolio and hired her.) Look how far she's come! It's so good to see people succeed (plus she is a pilot too).
Irene.

Irene had stimulated the lady in question to achieve the impossible. Today, the person Irene helped is not only a pilot, but she has gone on to own her own card and gift company. When you help someone else succeed, like Irene, you reap the reward of a sense of great achievement. Every day you meet lads that have great dreams. All that they need is someone like you to tell them they can do it. When you do that, you fuel them to attempt the impossible and achieve the unattainable!

The Worth of a Person's Life

If you forget everything you've just read, remember to answer the following questions: How do you want to be remembered? What have you done, or are you doing, to engrave a lasting legacy in the hearts of men and women you encounter every day? The worth of a person's life is not in the years he has lived, but in the impact those years have had on fellow human beings.

There is an interesting scene in Sylvester Stallone's movie, *Rambo*. Talking to the mercenaries who were sent to rescue the Christian missionaries in Burma, John Rambo challenges whether they were going to live for nothing or die for something. Influence is the knack of living for what you are willing to die for. It is better to be remembered for what you did or said with conviction, than to pretend to be politically correct and die a men's pleaser. It is better to error or to make mistakes in what you believe to be true, than to be successful in what you don't believe.

The worth of a person's life is in the inside of them. People may form opinions about other people. They may even be correct sometimes. But that does not change what is inside of people. Each person has inherent worth — no matter where they come from or what their background is. Social influence can alter that worth, but it cannot diminish it. People's opinion can temporarily silence that worth, but cannot kill it. When people are who they are, they have a greater chance to change society than when they want to behave against their good nature.

PART II

THE LAW OF PERSUASION

3

POWER OF CHANGED ATTITUDES

Leadership is the exertion of influence on people's attitudes in order to bring the best out of them.
— Charles Mwewa

Persuasion is when you influence someone else in your social setting to change his or her attitude. The goal of persuasion is to encourage the subject to make decisions that are reasonable. You don't merely inform people; you persuade them to turn from bad to good, from living a meaningless life to living a life full of purpose! Persuasion is fearlessness in the midst of confusion and uncertainties. It is to stand on your side even if others are skeptical. When people see that you are excited about what you believe in, they are persuaded to espouse your philosophy. Persuasion is power.

Attitudes Define People

An attitude is a positive or negative tendency towards people. It can also be towards events, actions, or practices. Whether it is towards a person, event, action, or practice attitudes can limit or maximize potential. Attitudes are born out of behavioral tendencies which have come to shape one's view of life and other people. When your attitude towards others is good, your approach and actions will be good as well. To change a person or people, change their attitudes first. Attitudes do change over time, due to many things, including individual experience. People who hold a certain view about life will likely behave in a similar fashion towards it.

Leadership exerts its influence on people's attitudes in order to bring the best out of them. You cannot successfully lead people who hold different views from yours. You first have to align their views to those you hold before leading them. Sharing the vision is the first step towards changing people's attitudes. People who have shared *into* your vision will bring the best results *out of* your vision. Those who either don't understand it, or are defiant to it, will make the vision stagnant.

In an organization, it is the duty of senior management to communicate and define the organizational vision to their subordinates. Communication must be simple, but aptly understood, so that the vision can be recited in well-chosen words. An organization that has not invested in this will reap the bitter reward of disillusionment among its employees. People join organizations for various reasons. They come from different backgrounds and orientations.

If you have ten people joining you, chances are you have ten different views and opinions coming into play. It is therefore the leader's job to harmonize all those variables into a well-understood objective. To do this, the leader must change or alter the people's attitudes. Changed attitudes are caused by changed behavior—and changed behavior will lead to increased performance.

The Power of Changed Attitudes

One remarkable thing about life is that we have a choice every day regarding the attitude we embrace for that day. Given all possibilities, man is most likely to side with wrong or to choose a twisted path. Some people are best led by strong persuasion. Persuasion is needed in life. To make profit, you need to persuade people about the product you are making or selling. To win an interview, you have to persuade your potential employer about your qualification and capability. To marry, you must persuade your fiancée or fiancé to marry you. So, whether you are just trying to win a friend, or convincing defiant factions to end conflicts by peaceful means, you need to exert some form of persuasion.

Persuasion is what shows man the right way to go. Influence is defined persuasion. All that you are doing when you persuade a person is influencing him or her to make the right decisions and do the right deeds. People sometimes do not know what they are supposed to do; they need to be influenced. Leadership is defined persuasive influence, because it involves the assertion of some directional, and even correctional, influence on people's attitudes and judgments.

Pointing the Way

When you persuade people, you are pointing the way. That is the role of leadership. A leader is someone who has been where he or she wants others to go. This may not mean being there personally, but through research and the experiences of others as well. Many people think that you need to have been there yourself to be able to successfully lead others. While that remains the conventional reasoning, leadership can also be acquired through observation, on-the-job training or via studying.

Usually good followers make great leaders. When you follow a leader, you begin to formulate mental concepts of successful leadership. You begin to see clearly what ought to, and doesn't need to be done. That is the best place to begin leadership: from following a leader. In other words, successful followership is the best prerequisite for successful leadership.

4

COMMUNICATION CLASSICS

*The basic building block of good
communication is the feeling that every
human being is unique and of value
—Charles Mwewa*

Every leader will be faced with the need to communicate effectively in order to influence his or her group. Speech is the commonest way of persuasion. Leadership thrives on speech. The basic building block of good communication is the feeling that every human being is unique and of value. This human uniqueness may pose a huge challenge because different people will behave differently. However, every form of public speaking with a practical purpose involves the ability to persuade.

Whether it is the kind of speech made by the chairman of the board to his colleagues, the kind of speech made by the proponent of a certain policy at a business conference, or the kind of speech made by one member of a household to the rest of the family, with the practical purpose of getting them to adopt a recommendation being advanced, the art of persuasion must be exploited.

In the classic expositions of practical rhetoric, from Aristotle and Plato to Cicero and Quintilian, practical speaking was enumerated under such headings as *deliberative* or political oratory, *forensic* or speech that occurs in judicial proceedings, as, for example, a lawyer's closing arguments to a jury, and *epidictic* or an effort to praise or dispraise something, whether that be a person or a policy. All these were forms of persuasion.

In everyday life there is always one form of persuasion or another being advanced. Thus, selling a product, or praising a person or a policy, are all efforts at what may be called *eulogistic* persuasion. It is no less obvious that political and forensic oratories are efforts to persuade the listeners to buy, say, a policy being advocated, a candidate being floated, or an evaluative judgment being promulgated.

The key to unlocking the willingness in your audience to accept a particular proposition lies in evoking favorable emotional impulses. Anyone doing this must bear in mind the recognition that all human beings have certain desires, such as desire for pleasure, honor, peace, freedom, justice, and etcetera. Persuaders must depend upon such desires being present and active motivating forces in almost all human beings.

Those persuading should take for granted that such desires exist. They should then call upon these desires for the objectives they have in mind. In doing so, they should concentrate on the reasons why the course of action recommended is a better way of gratifying them than some alternative that a competitor might be trying to present.

The leader's knowledge of his or her subject matter and the choice of words to evoke the emotive content of the hearers is important in tipping the scales in his or her favor. This is especially required if he or she is trying to make the products or service more desirable than those of the competitor or trying to make his or her candidate for public office preferable to an opponent's. This should be followed by giving the reasons why such products or services should be chosen.

One person I admire very much when it comes to public speaking is the evangelist Billy Graham. Billy Graham is perhaps the greatest emotional evoker I have ever listened to. His style is simple but very effective. He appeals to the challenges of everyday life and tailors his message to contemporary issues. After that he then gives a parallel to what the Bible says. Each time he throws the challenge to the crowd the responses are amazing. Billy utilizes the power of persuasion to his advantage. Sometimes a persuader doesn't need to induce emotions when the situation has already determined that.

In political campaigning or in a debate about conflicting policies the emotional appeal may be for the maintenance of peace, the defence of freedom or the securing of welfare benefits. In situation like these, persuaders do not have to create a desire for peace, freedom or welfare. The desire is already there to be used. Persuaders need only argue that their candidate or their policy serves that purpose better.

Persuaders cannot always count on desires that are generally prevalent in their audiences and ready to be brought into play.

Sometimes they must instill the very desire that they seek to satisfy with their policy or candidate. People have needs or wants that are dormant, needs or wants of which they are not fully aware. Persuaders must try to awaken and buoy these up. Sometimes they must try to create a desire that is new. Through words, they can stimulate dormant desires until they have aroused them and made them a driving force.

Unmasking Mark Antony

Mark Antony emerges from classical literature as one of the greatest persuaders of all time. After the brutal assassination of Julius Caesar at the hands of the Roman conspirators, led by Caesar's henchman, Marcus Brutus, Mark Antony was assigned the task of speaking last at Caesar's funeral. Antony caused a mutiny by eloquently persuading the audience to rise against the triumvirate. But what made this all remarkable was the image of Brutus presented to the Roman populace. Brutus was considered the favorite of Caesar's cohort, and the least likely to carry out such a brutal act against Caesar.

Mark Antony had a very difficult job. His task was to persuade the audience to believe that Brutus was capable of committing such a horrible act. He also had a task of convincing the audience that Brutus was the one who struck Caesar first. Mark Antony successfully aroused Rome's emotions, causing the people to vent their anger, abhorrence, and repugnance on Brutus and his comrades. Mark Antony, using the art of persuasion, was able to successfully sway Rome into mutiny.

When you consider contemporary leaders you cannot help but notice how they manage to win over difficult propositions. In recent years, George W. Bush led this horde of influencers. Every time he spoke about the war in Iraq, Americans were persuaded to allow him to sign more laws and channel more money towards the war efforts. President Bush could only do that because of very strong persuasive influence. It is amazing what strong influence can do. It can cause a nation or a community to blindly adopt a view, even if that view is wrong.

Consider politicians, it is the use of words that helps them share a dream, proposal a law, enact a statute, fend for their ridings or deceive the masses. Lawyers, church leaders, paralegals and so on, all utilize the power of persuasion to submit for a position. People are sometimes reluctant to do something unless persuaded to do so. Sometimes people have to be persuaded to do things which will eventually benefit them. Very little is accomplished without persuasion.

Old Strategy, Same Results

Perhaps the greatest speech influencer of his time was Barack Obama. When Obama appeared on the American political scene, he was hardly known. After the Iowa presidential primaries victory against John Edwards and Hillary Clinton, people suddenly began to take a second look at Obama. Within a period of less than eight months, Obama had revolutionized the way campaign fundraising was done in the United States of America and how grassroots organization was conducted.

If there was anything that Obama's opponents underestimated, it was not his race or longevity, or brevity, in the nation's Senate. It was the power of speech. Like Anthony, Obama's opponents were positively mistaken when they allowed him to speak to the American people. To cut the long story short, on January 20th, 2009, Obama was inaugurated as the first black president of the United States of America. Speech is the most effective weapon of influence. Speech cuts the soul, reshapes the mind, and moves the spirit. Speech is a real persuasive mechanism.

I have always wondered how spiritual leaders manage to raise large sums of money from the same people week in and week out. It is one thing to persuade people to contribute once, but to do so frequently surely takes some elevated kind of persuasive acumen. These men and women are quintessential persuaders who always succeed at moving the hearts of the people they encounter.

Good for Food; Pleasant to the Eye; Desirable for Wisdom

An interesting account is told in the Book of Genesis of how the serpent persuaded the first woman to break the commandment. The serpent intrigued the woman with his eloquence. But it was the strategy he employed that won him the day.

The old serpent utilized what is known in the classical Art of Rhetoric as *ethos* and *pathos*. The latter is concerned with emotions and the former with character. We have already mentioned the power of pathos (emotive content of the speech) in the previous sections.

The element of *ethos* may either precede or be combined with the employment of *pathos* in persuasive talk. The role of the serpent was to make himself look good, as well as to make the position he was advancing more desirable than what the Creator had to offer. Those in persuasion work for political candidates, for example, work in the same way. They try to paint a glowing picture of their candidate's character, in addition to activating the motives for subscribing to the policies for which he or she stands. Effective persuasion aims at advocating and advancing a preference for one product, one service, one position, one candidate, or one policy over another.

Human nature thrives on persuasion. You may have a talent, a gift, an ability or an idea. You may have a great dream. You may conceive a grand vision. You may even be famous and wealthy. But if you can't get people to know, like or follow you, you will remain but average. Even a great book will remain under the shelf if it is not advertised. People buy, follow and decide because they are presented with a choice. God put all His dreams and expectations for His creation in a Book. The primary purpose of writing down His views and ideas in the Bible was so that humans could be persuaded. You have a goal, a vision – persuade people to own it, and it will come to pass.

5

THE FEELING OF IMPORTANCE

No matter how sincere or how
melancholy they look, people have some
form of dream they pursue.
— *Charles Mwewa*

Whatever strategy is employed in persuasion, it cannot replace that of making people feel important. Make people feel important by listening to them and concentrating on what they are saying. People usually respond to leaders who they feel are genuinely interested in them. Have you ever wondered why certain people seem to attract the same people others fail to? I learned this when I took over a Sunday school class. Children are the best reference when it comes to attracting people.

Lessons from Sunday School Kids

We had a system of class rotations. Each week you were assigned to a different class from the one you had the previous week. I was surprised that kids had preferences. They liked certain teachers and not others. Parents of the children used to come to me saying that their child had been talking about me endlessly. Some kids would begin asking their parents as early as Tuesday to be brought to my class.

At first I thought kids just liked me because I brought them candy or sweets. But then I realized that even when I didn't give then candy, the kids still liked me. As I progressed in leadership, then I began to understand. All along I had made the kids feel important. I did simple things that I never even thought were important. But these are the very things that make great leaders great. Firstly, I smiled to the kids each time I entered the classroom. Kids, like every other human being, feel accepted when you smile at them. A smile is a powerful thing. It has a unique way of breaking barriers and creating amity among people.

Second, I remembered their names. In fact, one of my habits each time I was given a new class was to master the first names of at least fifty percent of the children the first day. Names are the greatest asset each person has. A person's name is to that person the sweetest and most important sound in any language. To address people by their names shows that you love them and that you care about them. If you want to prove this, just wait for your boss to call you by name in the group of many other employees. You will feel a sense of belonging. You'll go home with a sense of security that your company actually knows you. Everyone wants to be part of a group, not just part of a process.

Third, I listened to them. Human beings develop the ability to want to be listened to at a very tender age. When I entered the classroom, I asked each child how his or her day was. As each narrated, I listened and nodded my head. The child was encouraged to continue. But most importantly, the child felt important. You can imagine how excited the children were to learn that their views and stories, however unintelligible, were being listened to! Be a good listener. Your subordinates or friends will love you. They will know that you value their opinions and this will lead to increased performance and productivity.

Good listening is a virtue that will not only improve relationships but that will also give you an open window into the hearts of men. As you listen to people, you begin to know them better, to know what troubles them, and what their deepest needs are. Encourage others to talk about who they are. As people feel comfortable enough to speak to you, they will open up themselves to you, telling you facts and secrets only they can know.

I have listened to so many stories. I have helped thousands of people simply because they trusted me to know the depth of their hearts. That's how you can influence people. When you know that they have nothing to hide; and reciprocally, when they know that they can trust you, persuading them to take a particular path or change behavior will be a piece of cake!

Fourth, I talked to them in terms of their interests. This is the lesson you learn when you lead people: that however powerful your own vision is, people will come to you with their own secondary visions. I know of a man who had trouble integrating with his new company. The man was an excellent employee, a great performer. But his boss was too self-conscious. He wanted everyone to do or only say things that were in line with his vision.

At first, this will look like the obvious thing the boss needs to do. But leadership experience thinks the other way. No sooner do you insist on fulfilling only your vision than you frustrate that sense of destiny in others. Every person has interests, what we may call desires. No matter how sincere or how melancholy they look, people have some form of dream they pursue.

The best way to motivate people is to give them the impression that in fulfilling your master vision, they will be nearing theirs as well. How do you do this? Definitely not by sermonizing or denouncing their vision! You simply talk to people in terms of their interests. You ask personal questions. You find out how you can be of help to them. You genuinely become interested in their dreams, aspirations, and desires. You suggest ways of fulfilling those aspirations, and you provide the necessary inspiration they need to succeed.

When you give your best for others, others will return the best to you. If you want to have loyal and honest employees or subordinates, be trustworthy and dedicated to them. The best leader is the one who regards his or her position as a privilege more than a right!

The other day Roland, one of our men, came to me with a compliment. He had been touched by my leadership style. He told me that I was the first person to take him seriously in all his entire life. Because of his extroverted nature, most people, including those who led him before me, thought he was unbalanced. I disregarded other people's opinions and looked at him as he could be. When you treat people as they could be, they become as they should be! Today he does us proud. He heads our publicity department and does a remarkable job.

Appreciation—Deepest Human Principle

When you persuade people, you are in fact advising them to say or think the right way. In order words, you are influencing their attitudes. A good leader desires to change people without giving offense or even arousing bitterness. Do you often wonder why successful leaders seem to attract strong personalities around them? A leader is a leader because he or she has followers. Without faithful and loyal followers the role of a leader is undefined. Thus a leader puts a lot of premium on people because they define his role.

People often do not like confrontations. They would prefer being praised or appreciated for what they say or do. This is the easiest way of winning people to your side. People resist change when they suspect that coercion or intimidation is at play. To persuade them successfully you have to appeal to their sense of worth and importance. They need to feel appreciated and as being an integral part of the process, and not only as the means to the end. And this is the biggest mistake most leaders make. After they have led and won the group's confidence, they begin to take the group for granted. People put a certain limit on tolerance. And the difficulty is that you may not know when they have reached that limit. The result will be rebellion, and justifiably so!

Leading human beings is a complex responsibility. When I began leading people, I learned very early that certain principles underlined successful leadership. As I led, I began to make some trophy-winning observations. One of these happened when a certain member of my group seemed to call attention to what he had done. He wanted everyone to know what he had personally accomplished. At first, I was naïve and necessarily wanted to stop this sort of behavior for fear it would spread to the others. But then I realized that he derived great satisfaction in doing what he did. I reasoned that stopping that attitude would injure his self-esteem.

So, I resorted to praising the slightest improvement I saw in him. After I did this, he naturally went on improving and bringing results. Inside all of us is the craving for appreciation and praise for what we have accomplished. An insensitive leader will ignore this quality, but successful leaders utilize it to their advantage. Praise every improvement in your workers, subordinates, or followers. Be hearty in your approbation and lavish praise where it is due. The deepest principle in human nature is the craving to be appreciated. Don't criticize, condemn, or complain. Give honest and sincere appreciation. When you do this, you will get a very loyal and enthusiastic group, keen to bring you results.

6

PERSUASIVE INFLUENCE

*People are best persuaded when they feel
that love or genuine concern is the
motive, not power or force.*
— Charles Mwewa

Public speakers utilize different strategies in dealing with different situations. There is a method for person-to-person talk and another for more than one person. Naturally, the job of persuading one person is lighter than that of persuading an audience. Politicians, business executives, and clergymen are frequently faced with situations in which they have to address large audiences. Each of these people may have different messages for their audiences, but the philosophy underlying the presentation is the same. They are persuading their audiences to vote, buy into a particular policy, obey a commandment, or perform certain obligations.

Persuasive Angles

Having been in the public-speaking business for some time, I have observed how audiences display certain attitudes to different messages presented before them. The first attitude the audience may display is that of being pro-message. The audience is already in favor of the message being communicated. This is usually common in situations where there has been adequate publicizing of the meeting. This happens a lot in religious gatherings and political rallies.

Conveners of the meeting would have already promoted the subject of the particular meeting or conference so that the audience is already aware and interested in the message. I have been invited to meetings where the theme has been communicated to me. Practically everyone is aware of the subject matter. The job of the persuader or speaker in this case is simply to advocate a position that the audience is already favorable towards.

Sometimes, you may step onto the platform and discover that the audience already agrees with your position. This situation makes the work of persuasion simpler. It is much easier to persuade people who are already in agreement with your position. This happens a lot at political party conventions. Usually cadres or political devotees come to these meetings to endorse a position. This situation calls for message sidedness. The audience will applaud each time you reinforce their position, and mumble when you deviate from it. The audience's behavior may guide you into a path that will lead to maximum persuasion.

The Philosophy behind Persuasive Techniques

People have done things they would not have done had it not been for persuasion. People have bought things, volunteered their services, and donated to certain causes simply because someone effectively persuaded them to. But sometimes people have been warped, abused, or even been made to lose property because of the same. So whether one uses them to influence others positively or negatively, persuasive techniques work. Companies are now investing enormous amounts of money in advertisement. Most of these ads are based on strong persuasive techniques which are meant to sway the masses for commercial purposes.

Marketing agencies use the theory that repeated exposure to a persuasive message may increase acceptance. Haven't you switched off your television set because you did not like a particular ad, only to be captivated by the same another time? This is the reason why ads are overtly repeated! Because when you keep listening to a persuasive message, you will end up accepting it. Some people may term it brainwashing, but the principles are the same. People tend to like, in the long run, what they keep hearing, even if they didn't like it the first time.

Another technique used in marketing and advertising is the use of a person or people who are likely to command some sort of credibility. People are most likely to be persuaded by people they believe to be highly credible with respect to what they are talking about, based on their expertise, trustworthiness, or popularity. Other techniques include physical attractiveness, pleasantness, similarity to the audience, likeability, and so on. It is believed that those who may not be drawn to hearing a persuasive message for any reason, may do so upon seeing or hearing an attractive person.

The Best Way

Power is rarely a lasting way of influencing people. People may agree simply because they are threatened with punishment or because they are promised something. I learned a harsh lesson when we were setting up the *World Influence Vision* in Toronto in around 2006. I tried to win people mostly by promising things. What I discovered was that when those promises were fulfilled, people left. And, worse still when we didn't live up to those promises, they left again. At first I thought there was something wrong with my personality or character. It was none of that. I merely used a weak method of persuasion—and a costly one, too. People are best persuaded when they feel that love or genuine concern is the motive, not power or force.

Milk for My Daughter

Getting people to behave in a way we want them to is a persuasive aspect of social relations. We comply with subtle and situational cues that are arranged to increase our likelihood of agreeing to a request, almost on a daily basis. This is mostly done by people with no particular authority over us.

I remember when I was writing this book, sitting at my laptop, busily typing. My daughter, Emmerance, wanted some milk from the fridge. She first came and demanded that I give it to her. But, being busy, I declined. After some time, I saw her come again—this time she was so sweet to me that I couldn't resist the opportunity to do her a favor. So, even though I was busy, I left what I was doing and gave her the milk. I was persuaded by her sweet influences.

Dining to Win

Have you ever wondered why great contracts have been concluded over lunch or dinner? People tend to be in a good mood when they are eating. The biblical tale of two brothers, Esau and Jacob, illustrates this point. When the two boys were growing up, Esau, the older of the two, was a skillful hunter, and Jacob was a mild man who dwelled in tents. One day Jacob cooked stew, and Esau came from the field, very tired. Esau asked Jacob for some stew, but Jacob refused, insisting Esau sell him his birthright for food. Esau, reasoning that he was about to die and that his birthright would mean nothing when he was dying, went ahead and sold his birthright to his brother.

Most businesses and companies "sell" their birthrights over a plate of food. It is a human weakness to be relaxed a little bit when eating. And people are equally persuaded when you say something nice about them. This is known as the art of ingratiation. People's behavior changes when they are ingratiated.

Again, Emmerance has used this technique so well to get a favor from me. I remember one day I was busy again on my laptop, preparing a speech. Emmerance, knowing that I hate to be disturbed when I was working, came and touched me, mumbling a few kind words here and there, and then pressed my hand to take her to the fridge. Again I obliged.

Ingratiation Techniques

Men have used ingratiating techniques to win over women since the beginning of time. What we call a marriage proposal is nothing but asking for a marital favor by saying something nice about the lady. Wise men utilize ingratiation to their advantage. It is a beautiful thing to paint a picture, through words, of what you want. Only an unwise person would go to a lady and say little or nothing about her. It empowers women to consent, and do so with joy. It is in every girl, every woman, to feel good about herself when a man ingratiates himself. Men have a task, not only to ingratiate themselves with their women, but also to do so sincerely.

Flattery is another ingratiation technique commonly used especially in persuading "lofty" personalities. I know one guy who loved to be flattered. Every time, after a speaking engagement, he would ask me, "Charles, how did I do?" Would I say, "Bad, average, needs improvement"? Oh, no! I would butter him up, even though he was naturally a good speaker.

National leaders, top executives, and people in power have been flattered since time immemorial. Flattery is also a great technique if you want to obtain a favor from a reluctant person. However, some people take offense when they are flattered. It is advisable to use this persuasive gimmick only when you are sure you know what kind of a person you are dealing with.

Get Some, Give Some

Returning favor, or what social psychologists call a reciprocity norm, is a persuasive technique which has been in use for a very long time. It is kind of rule that is very hard to break. It is done by asking for a favor more valuable than what you do for the other. Charitable organizations use this by sending you a little something and asking for your donation in return.

Once I received a pack of name and address labels from an organization dealing with sight vision in Ontario. An enclosed note first described what the organization was all about and how it helped people through the generous support of people like me. Then, as if what would follow was not important, the organization's chief executive officer appended a plea: "The enclosed labels are a gift, our way of thanking you in advance for your gift…" That is exactly an example of a reciprocity norm. By giving you a little something, they touch your heart for your bigger donation. Most people consider this technique very humane.

Sometimes you may be asked for a small favor in order to get something big. That's what happened when I won a trip to Las Vegas. I was contacted by a certain agency which asked me to subscribe to a particular program yearly, and in turn I won a package to the "entertainment capital" of the world. Ask me, if there hadn't been any such enticement, whether I would have bothered, and the answer is no. We are mostly persuaded when we believe that an action demanded of us will be profitable to us immediately or in future.

False Truths or True Lies

Call them true lies or false truths—when your child comes to you and asks you for a thousand dollars; take it from me, he or she means one hundred dollars. What the child is doing is *opening the door in your face* by asking for a larger favor first, then the small.

What happened when you were growing up—you were in a group among your peers and prom day was around the corner? You saw this immaculate dress that you believed was perfect for the occasion. The dress cost two hundred and thirty dollars. But you knew that your mom would give you less than that if you mentioned the actual price. So you went to your mom and suggested that the dress you saw cost four hundred dollars. By suggesting a larger price you believed that your mom would give you less than that but enough to purchase the dress! This technique is used a lot in corporate budgeting. Department heads will ask for larger sums of moneys than they need with a belief that what is actually needed will be granted.

That's-Not-All Technique

If you are a late night stocker then you have had some opportunity to listen to the flowery language of infomercials. The principle behind this technique is to give you the impression that what is being offered has been austerely lowered. A product costs thirty dollars. The technique is to show you that if you purchase it at twenty dollars, you will then get ten dollars' worth of extras. You are meant to believe that you are buying something at a much more reduced price than what is usual. But actually you are only paying the real price.

Gospel ministers persuade potential converts in a similar way. "If you accept Jesus, then you will also receive peace, salvation…" is a very common device employed in evangelistic campaigns. The listener is made to understand that receiving Jesus has added benefits. This technique has a causation element to it—that one act happens as a direct result of another. In other words, performing the first operation will result in another and more desirable outcome.

In Bed with a Wrong Person

Nothing hurts like waking up to learn that you have been made to sign the wrong documents. By that, I mean, to discover that you've made the wrong choice, by right means. Let me illustrate this by an incident that happened to me. I am an eBay enthusiast, and I have bought all kinds of things from the Internet superstore.

This particular day, I was on the Internet, shopping for a rocking chair for my daughter, Tashany-Idyllia. Without paying attention to details, I bid and won what I believed to be a beautiful chair. Two weeks later the item arrived. But, to my surprise, it came in a small box. What immediately ran into my mind was that I had received a surprise parcel. Opening it, I was shocked to learn that it was the rocking chair I had won on eBay. What happened to the chair I thought I had won? Was I tricked by eBay? Not at all! I made a conscientious choice without paying attention to details. What I thought was a normal rocking chair turned out to be a toy. When I went back to check the details, there it was, including the fact that it was only a miniature rocking chair.

Have you read a newspaper lately? Observed something? Perhaps you will be amazed to learn that people have made many wrong choices based on faulty premises. Some of these choices could have been prevented with a little bit of attention to details. So how do you wake up with the wrong man in bed? People are persuaded to make choices they would not deny they did, but which they are loath. This is usually achieved through a technique I call "In Bed with a Wrong Man" or the "Irony of Fine Print." How does this work?

You are first bombarded with details of great news, usually in bold capital-lettered prints. All that you see is the offer and the amazing benefits of buying the product. But what you overlook are the tiny conditions written at the bottom of the page. Or, if it is on television, similar conditions will run on very fast, that, unless you are attentive, you may not hear. After you've ordered the product or service, then you come to be told that there are conditions. If you thought you were paying half price then you come to learn that such an offer was only possible if you had performed some other actions. Many people would simply end up paying the full amount considering how far they have already come.

People also are persuaded when they feel that their freedom of choice is threatened. This is achieved through sinister methods like censoring an item. When people are made to believe that an item, such as a book, has been censored, they are persuaded to desire it. Psychologically, people think that a censored item should have certain knowledge no one wants them to know. This feeling itself is a great motivator for possessing the item. It is human nature to crave something we believe is scarce or difficulty to obtain. The belief that an item is scarce produces in us a feeling of ecstasy for the item in limited supply. Some suppliers go to the extent of pretending the item is out of stock. This also explains why we hanker after antiques.

7

COMFORMITY INFLUENCE

*It appears that the world's brightest
persuaders are the greatest leaders as well
— Charles Mwewa*

Have you ever wondered why people obey? Where do people get the willingness to do what they are told? One theory is that *proximity* plays a pivotal role. People obey due to proximity to the victim, to authority, or to institutional setting. Relationships are very important in leadership. One time I asked a leader of a certain international organization what he thought was the most important factor in unswerving obedience to authority by subordinates. His answer was: relationships. By creating close and sincere relationships with your subordinates and colleagues, you are not only drawing them close to your side, but are winning their hearts to you as well. People who feel that they are part of a course usually give more of themselves to it.

Obedience Theories

People also obey due to *conformity pressure*. Wisdom says that when you strike the shepherd the sheep will scatter. The opposite is also true: gain the leader and the followers will gather! This theory is based on the premise that if you make leaders obey, others will simply follow. The saying that everything stands and falls on leadership hangs firm here. I remember our leader bringing us numerous guest speakers when I served under a Christian ministry. One particular speaker brought a very strange message, the kind which bordered on untested philosophical thinking. Most of us didn't agree with the speaker's views. But we all did what the speaker told us to do because our leader did. The same thing happens in business, or companies where the leader endorses a process or product, and everyone simply obeys. We can also term this as *blind obedience*.

This is where leaders should be careful. While serving as a youth director, I observed how the young people were affected by my life. They literally accepted everything I said without question. I noticed that they tried to imitate everything

I said, the way I said it, and my attitude towards such things. This too is true of movie celebrities and sports superstars. These are idolized to the extent that everyone follows what they say or do without question.

During the 2002 Soccer World Cup, the Brazilian soccer superstar Ronaldo shaved his hair in an unorthodox fashion. The following week his style had already become popular. Leaders, and all those in influential positions, have a huge responsibility to make sure that their behavior and actions do not mislead young people. But they also have a rare opportunity of using their influence to persuade people to live up to certain standards!

People also obey due to gender, cultural differences, and personality traits. Certain messages favor women more than men. And some people may find it hard to obey someone of a different culture from theirs. Some people are likeable or sociable. Some personalities may hinder people from obeying. In my leadership experiences I have come across people who totally reject me, even before they hear me speak.

I have also come across people who just like my style and are willing to listen to me. I try to persuade even those who don't seem to like me. Sometimes I succeed, while other times I fail. But in whatever situation I find myself, I try to convince my audience that what I am saying is worthy for them to hear. I aim at persuading them to listen and accept my message.

I remember very vividly a town called Ndola, in Zambia, where I was the guest speaker to a certain group. When I was introduced, many people showed disapproval, and even disappointment. I was young, and most of the people in the crowd were older than me. I felt humiliated. I had two options, though: fold my tail and go, or stand up to the challenge.

Usually when you are speaking to a group, there is one enemy you must conquer, called stage fright. But in this case I had also to conquer the audience's apathy. I put my dilemma aside and decided to speak anyway. Just about five minutes into my message, I began to see a change. Suddenly, all those who were showing signs of resentment began to sit straight up in their seats. Those who were fidgeting and shuffling their feet stopped. There was a total silence which was followed by an outburst of ululations and a standing ovation. I had immediately become a local hero. One man after the meeting came to my hotel room and apologized.

Sometimes people may not be persuaded by your physical appearance or age. But you can use the other instruments at your disposal. This is the same reason that some people are very effective as radio announcers but not as television presenters. People may like one's voice and ideas but hate one's appearance and vice versa. There are no limits to the strategies you can use to influence people. The secret is to discover what works well for you and utilize it to your advantage.

The Inevitability of Leadership Persuasion

Leadership is the art of persuading people. Business leaders, political leaders, church leaders and leaders of charities all thrive on persuasion. Neglecting this art might mean being out of business or out of favor with people. Voluntary organizations especially need the art of persuasion in order to remain in business. Whether you are in charge of thousands, or four people, you will need to know how to persuade them.

Every leader must persuade his or her people to stay committed to the vision of the organization. Simply repeating slogans or wishing well will not do. Creatively persuade your group to take particular actions. Start by asking small then move on to big. Follow up a big request after someone makes a donation by reminding them of the previous gesture. I know of a church organization that has been undertaking a multi-million building project. And the challenge has been finances. What better a time to motivate people towards giving? And nothing can do this better than persuasion.

The Unquenchable Thirst for Influencers

There are people out there who are waiting for you to influence them in a positive way. Leadership is influencing people in a way that allows them to live meaningful lives and maximize their potentials. Taking a closer look at history, we find a renowned retinue of remarkable leaders who have embraced national records. Corax of Syracuse emerges eminent among them. He was the actual founder of rhetoric as a science in the 5th Century B.C and he defined rhetoric as the "artificer of persuasion." He expressly enumerated the efficacy of using persuasive arguments in establishing probable truth where absolute truth could not be proved.

It appears that the world's brightest persuaders are the greatest leaders as well. Antiphon, Isocrates, Plato, Aristotle, Demosthenes, Cicero, Edmond Burk, Daniel Webster, Abraham Lincoln, Sir Winston Churchill, Martin Luther King, Jr., Mahatma Gandhi, Kofi Annan, Nelson Mandela, Frederick Chiluba, to mention but a few, were not just great leaders, but were also masters of persuasion.

PART III

THE KIND LAW OF CARING

8

CARING ADVANTAGE

Show me a real champion, a real-life
winner, and I will show you a person
who lives by example and shows others
how to win.
— *Charles Mwewa*

The Kind Law of Caring put simply, states that be kind to people and care about them. This is antithetical to being mean and individualistic. Society has never run short of the "caring professionals"—men and women who have been trained to earn a living by providing care. Caring cannot be intellectual because true care comes from the depth of the heart. Everyone has the capacity to care, to love someone heartily, and render a service that eases another's pain or suffering. Caring involves the following five aspects, what I call the Five Facets of Caring:

Responding to the Needs and Concerns of Others

The first facet of caring involves responding to the needs and concerns of others. To do this successfully you must first know what those needs and concerns are. There are some obvious cases or scenarios in which you easily pick out what concerns and troubles people. For instance, if you walk along any busy downtown street in winter, you cannot help but feel compassion for the homeless without shelter. Other times, it is not very obvious what people's needs are. But research and study can help. Knowing people's needs causes you to respond in some positive way, to help or alleviate the need.

Knowing about people's needs is, however, not enough; it should take both feeling for them and acting in their interest. That sense of empathy is what triggers certain energies in us to rise to the occasion and help. The challenge most of us face, when it comes to caring for others, is that we want to wait until we feel. Usually that will take forever to happen. We can, in the interest of care, consult everything in us and do something for the needs around us.

Sensitivity to the Needs and Concerns of Others

The second facet of caring involves being sensitive to the needs and concerns of others. Some people will never tell us what troubles them. But is it hard to understanding the care needs of others? Not at all! People may not say what troubles them, or what their needs are, but they may act in ways that show it. They may even say things that point to their need for care. These clues may be in the form of complaints, suggestions, simple remarks, etcetera, but they will be sufficient to help us know the particular need or concern. Being sensitive also means being attentive to what is not said, and perceptive to what is not mentioned.

Sensitivity in caring for others is a human response to helping others thrive. It is a thoughtful gesture and a true expression of the human conscience. What nobler cause than to be able to contribute to the well-being and success of others! And yet that's exactly what you are doing when you care for others. You are helping them cope, flourish, and prosper. You are making a real difference in the lives of others.

My family and I have opened our doors to people in dire need. We have accommodated colleagues and friends and have provided unprecedented care. Perhaps the most care we have pertinently provided is to HIV/AIDS-afflicted people we know. Because of stigmatization of the victims of the pandemic, most people do not wish to disclose their status, except to the people they truly trust. We love these people and accept them the way they are. We also try to accommodate them in the best possible way whenever we can. Sometimes it is risky, but that is what definite care is all about.

In the year 2001 a young man came to ask me if I could help him with his school-fee obligations. As my custom has always been, I first wanted to know him better and understand his situation. I did a background check and discovered that Marvin (not his real name) was a double orphan and was living with an abusive uncle. He was on the verge of losing his place in school and needed serious help.

I did not only help him financially, I also took him in as a member of my household. Under my care, he completed his secondary education and went on to study theology. All this happened because I cared. You may not know what will become of the person you render your care to. And yet there is nothing more fulfilling than caring for someone without expecting anything in return!

Treating People with Kindness

The third facet of caring involves treating people with kindness. Caring is not just a way of feeling; it is also a way of behaving. You show you are a caring person by doing caring things. Doing caring things means responding with kindness and doing particular deeds. When you meet a senior person attempting to cross the road and you offer to help, you are behaving kindly.

People who donate blood and human body parts are kind, showing a type of kindness that is practical and pragmatic. The movie *John Q,* starring Denzel Washington, is the best illustration of the significance of donors. In this movie, John Q's son is saved by the heart of a donor who died in a road accident. The donor was

kind enough to allow the use of her heart in
the occasion of her demise.

Giving Yourself for the Benefit of Others

The fourth facet of caring involves
giving yourself for the benefit of others.
The example of the donor above is
consistent with the fourth facet of caring.
When my two daughters were born, at the
Scarborough General hospital in Ontario, I
witnessed both deliveries. In both cases, I
was touched by the kindness of the nurses.
One particular nurse in Emmerance's case
was so caring that I do not know what I
would have done without her.

Emmerance is our first-born girl. At the
time of her birth, neither Clarice nor I had
any experience in childbirth. The nurse
patiently and lovingly showed us; by doing
everything we needed to kick-start our
parenting. You and I know that it is the
nurses' duty to do what they are trained for.
But in this case, she went beyond simply
fulfilling her payroll conditionality, to
actually caring as she would for her own
child.

You don't need to be a firefighter, a
soldier in harm's way, or a social worker to

care for others. All you need is just to give yourself to the benefit of others. You can volunteer your free time to care for the elderly in homes, visit terminally ill patients in hospitals, or help in the rehabilitation of substance abusers. You can say kind words to someone and people will cheer; but when you share yourself for another person, you truly care.

Charitable Involvements

The fifth, and final, facet of caring involves the work of charity—the convenient assistance of the needy with practical help. Charities do remarkable jobs. The good works of aid organizations complement the effort by governments to help care for different needs. The best you can do is to donate your money or services to these charities. In doing this you are contributing to the betterment of many lives. You are expressing your caring in a practical way. The next time you hear about an opportunity to give for charitable causes, be caring enough to answer the call. Doing this is one of the ways you share yourself and your energy.

The people you touch through your charitable deeds may never even know your name. But you are a hero in every respect. Because when these needy people, who may include children and the elderly, are helped, it might mean they are rescued from pain, disease, poverty, ignorance, and even death. The best life to brag about is one which was lived for others, through contribution and caring. And what better way to do so than to join in charitable causes!

Caring is the reason why I serve as board chairman of Mission Music Inc. (Mission). Mission uses music to raise funds in order to help AIDS orphans in Africa. There are many precious children in Africa and in other parts of the world who need practical care. Through organizations like Mission, you can join the force of caring men and women who are helping to assuage pain, suffering and death through their care. In life, the greatest truth is in realizing that the help you give to others through care is not a choice you make, but a debt you owe your fellow human beings.

9

THE WISDOM OF WINNING

By setting a good example and helping
another to win, that is how you will also
win.
— *Charles Mwewa*

You can do deeds, and say words, and influence people. But only deeds done and words said with compassion have the force of permanently affecting people. Compassion begins with sympathy and ends with empathy. When you seek to understand and consider the limitations of others, you are compassionate. Compassion is the basis of servitude. True servants of the people are those who compassionately get into other people's shoes and try to understand the challenges those people face and the pain they endure. Compassion eliminates all forms of selfishness and places others above self.

Most people who have influenced their world, and left a mark on life, are and were compassionate people. Compassionate people have a sharing comportment and a caring deportment. Compassionate people tilt their ears towards the poor, the sick and vulnerable individuals. They are moved by compassion to administer justice and goodwill to men.

The Excellence of Caring

One of the characteristics of men and women who have influenced their world and left a mark on life is their ability to care. The *excellence of caring*, as I prefer to call it, is a rare quality some people have. The ability to care always seems to be preceded by some form of pain or sacrifice. Consider mothers: the pain of childbirth leave them with an extraordinary capacity for caring. Basically, we all care for those things we perceive to represent a particular degree of value. Usually that value is acquired by making tremendous sacrifices.

How does the caring mentality come about? Let me answer this by reference to a lottery or gambling. When someone wins a lottery, he or she becomes an instant millionaire. Every day people are winning large sums of money through gambling. But when you look at the lives of these people, they seem to lack direction and purpose. This happens even in spite of the enormity of the finances they have.

But consider the lives of genuine millionaires, men and women who have what they have due to hard work and sacrifice. They live balanced lives, full of purpose and meaning. They also seem, more than gambling millionaires, to care for what they have. Why is it like that? It is because when you achieve something by sacrifice and pain you treasure it more and therefore care for it more. The pain of acquiring is the gain you treasure. Sacrifice gives way to celebration.

Distill to Instill

Caring for others is not a one-time hit. It grows as you consistently give of yourself to the service and benefit of the needy. It can be compared to the distillation of wine. You look at wine, and ask yourself: where did they distil such a fine product? You may be surprised to learn that it was from rough grapes. But what the brewer did was to take those rough grapes and prepare them through numerous processes until it had become perfect.

Like rough grapes, life is also as a raw, rough piece of wood. One may look at it and see only something fit for firewood. But a curio maker will see it as a potential piece of fine furniture or work of art. Do not be afraid to refine those qualities that are natural to you, especially those of kindness and caring. Potential is useless until it is exercised. Consider the generation of hydro power. Water has a latent energy called potential. At this latent stage it is useless and innocuous. But, given a push, it is transformed into kinetic energy which leads to the generation of power.

We all have the capacity to care or succeed in life. In short, we have the potential. For most people, unfortunately, this potential dies with them because it was never translated into a moving energy. That's why we began *Win-Again Newsletter*. At Win-Again, we didn't create the potential in people—it was already inherent in them. All we did was simply give a push. This push might come in the form of an urge, an encouragement, a piece of advice, or an inspired quote. We motivated people to act on their potential and turn it into a driving force. We translated people's potential success into kinetic success. This was the true meaning of empowerment.

There is power in letting go. Steve Hawke, who played the role of European Tarzan in the years 1969 to 1970, is an acquaintance of mine, and he told me a fascinating story. He said a certain man had pretended all his life to be a preacher. One day this preacher embarked on a fishing trip with his friends. There arose a sudden storm in the middle of the lake. Their boat began to capsize. And because the preacher did not know how to swim, he started to drown.

One of his colleagues shouted: "*Give* me your hand!" But the drowning man refused. The friend repeated, "Let out your hand or else you will perish!" The man again refused, and he died. When she heard about her dear husband's death, the preacher's wife enquired, "Did you try to save him?"

"On two occasions," they answered. "We asked him to *give* us his hand, and he refused."

"Oh, no!" exclaimed the wife. "That man always wanted to *get*. You should have told him to *receive* yours, instead," she said.

What's the moral of the short story? It is an illustration on how those who refuse to give care also fail to receive it. When you give, you receive. The man in the story only knew how to get; he didn't know how to give. He perished because he withheld. When you give, you live. This is what care is. The people you give your care to, do live. Are there loyal hearts? Are there spirits brave? Are there souls that are true and pure? Then show the world you care, and the best will always come in your care!

This is How to Win

People think they know how to win. Some believe chance has a lot do with it. The courageous ones believe is it hard work and determination. And both are correct. But there is another way of winning I would like you to know. Inspire confidence in others and lead them by example. Sincerely and tirelessly help others to win in life. By setting a good example and helping another to win, that's how you will also win. Caring for another, whether that be a member of your immediate family, a neighbor, a relative or a total stranger, is the best way of helping others to win in life.

10

CARING LEADERSHIP

Leadership is the art of caring.
— *Charles Mwewa*

Leadership should be a caring affair. A leader has people around him or her who have diverse aspirations and dreams. His or her role is to direct, harmonize, and augment this diversity into a performing force. As a custodian of dreams and aspirations, a leader must exhibit caring tendencies in the discharge of his or her leadership duties. Below are ten characteristics that define a caring leader.

#1 Caring Leaders are Servants

When Jesus was nearing his death, he gathered his disciples and taught them what true leadership means. He washed their dirty feet. In our times, washing people's feet is a duty relegated to low servants. Bosses shouldn't be bending down washing their subordinates' dirty feet, we think. But in actuality, the shortest route to greatness is in serving others. You may not wash your subordinates' feet like Jesus did, but you can lead by example.

#2 Caring Leaders Earn Respect

They don't demand it. Leaders who love the grandeur of titles usually do not live up to expectations. I don't mind being called by my first name. What I mind is being labeled an ineffective, non-caring leader. To some people, it all ends in big titles. Such types love to be addressed by their elegant titles: chief, bishop, general manager, CEO, president, etcetera. There is nothing wrong with being called by all these titles if performance and caring are the motives. Most people who influenced their world were not even elected to any position or office.

#3 They Bring Higher Social Returns

They serve society as a whole. They are not only there for themselves and their families; they go out of their ways to affect different levels of existence. They desire no personal glory; they work for the good of all. Caring leaders have sacrificed their own comforts and safety for the sake of the entire nation. Think of freedom fighters, human rights activists, and so many men and women who labor for the common good. Think of selfless men and women who have built our nations on their sweat and blood. And now think about these men and women as leaders, and caring ones, for that matter.

#4 Caring Leaders are People-Oriented

Medical doctors spend substantial amounts of time caring for their patients. Most of them rarely spend quality time with their own families. They go to all this trouble because they love people. Their work not only is centered on people, but is also very demanding. Doctors, like most men and women who have had an impact on their world, are people-oriented. Everything they do and say is centered on the good of humanity. By their word and deed, great civilizations have been built; and by their selfless sacrifices others have entered the portals of power.

#5 Caring Leaders are Invisible

That is, they like to keep their contributions confidential. When they give to charitable causes, they don't create a publicity stunt out of it. Our world is ruled by greedy leaders who are bent on saving their own faces. They have created media machines which publicize all of their doings. Sometimes you might think they are the only ones who are making a difference. Real heroes are even unheard of, and yet they are invincible—and these include ordinary men and women who go out of their way to touch others in meaningful ways. It could even be you reading this book.

#6 Caring Leaders Touch the Core of Man

They refresh the soul and warm the heart. That's what makes them significant because they reach to where it matters most. They take time to care as if everything depended on it. You can see it in their deeds, and perceive it in their words. They don't just do more, they give out all. They are the Mother Theresas of our time. And wherever they are, lives are touched and society is changed for good.

#7 Caring Leaders Leave Lasting Legacies

Caring leaders leave behind a legacy that outlives them. Even after they die, their influence lingers on and affects people's actions, behaviors, beliefs, and attitudes. Caring leaders realize that life is too precious and too short to be wasted. They know that no one has the ability to live forever. So they endeavor to excel in their domains, or sphere of influence, where their life story is inscribed.

You can't do everything, but you can do one thing and do it really well. It's possible to change the world, but the world cannot all be changed at once. That's why the idea of domains is very important. There is an area in which you can do better, a domain you are wired to bring under control. The first job you have is to define your domain. It could be religious, political, social, academic, legal, scientific, technological, or otherwise. Once it is defined, begin to plant yourself there, by studying what ought to be known about the area and then exerting your influence therein. Once you've discovered your domain, aim at excelling in it and aim to be the best you can be.

Caring leaders synergize every moment. If you are a boxing fan, as I am, then you must be aware of the importance of not wasting punches. Whether it is a combination of jabs or a single uppercut, every blow in the ring counts towards the final score. But any boxer will also tell you that he or she wishes for that one moment when an opening will present itself. And it is at such a moment that a knockout is scored.

Synergy is strength in a synchronized moment. In other words, it is achieving the results of many moments in one. Others will term this *Moment Maximization*. An appropriate time is a synergy of many factors gone before. Moments are relative. There are moments for each action under the sun. Moments could be short or long. Moments could be sad or happy. Moments can bring pleasure or ennui.

Caring leaders make the best of every moment. They take every moment seriously, because they never know which one would take someone into their destiny. Remember that small steps add up to a mile. One's moment could be just helping a senior citizen cross the road or could be to organize a fundraising event for the fight against cancer or AIDS. Whatever the moment is, it shouldn't be despised. This is the same reason you don't have to look down on small things and insignificant beginnings.

Anyone who dreamed a world-changing dream began it in the shadow of his or her heart. It was small and insignificant. But the difference came when the dream was put into action. Caring people do not ignore small signs of destiny. They don't neglect talent, either. They know that it is small efforts which lead to a whole. A businessman who makes smaller, but steady, profit is better off than another who is waiting to make a one-time gigantic leap! And influence is often pummeled from moment synergizing.

#8 Caring Leaders are Trailblazers

They are trailblazers who begin something from nothing. Caring leaders are not magic workers; they simply take advantage of needs to create strategic solutions to ameliorate them. Take the case of the HIV/AIDS: while some are still floundering over stigmatization and moral consequences, caring leaders are already fashioning strategies to help victims survive. They are lobbying governments and financial institutions, and raising awareness. They do this because they see an opportunity to help, to show kindness, and demonstrate care in a real way. They think positive and see a way even where there seems to be none.

You can bet caring leaders won't spend their time rabble-rousing. That's too parochial for their stamina. They channel their useful energy towards inventing solutions. They exhibit a caring mentality for nature and for what they may not call theirs. Even the Bible entreats people to care for the things that are not theirs. If you are faithful with another man's enterprise, you can be trusted with your own as well. And if you can care for small things, you can equally care for large ones.

A caring mentality extends kindness and help in a way that is useful to the person being cared for. It strives to provide a platform where those who need care can actualize themselves and be self-reliant when the source of such care diminishes. In turn, this kind of attitude helps victims and becomes a force that enhances their life experience. To care for people is to help them grow and actualize themselves. It is to be concerned and to actually facilitate the growth and actualization of the people you care for.

#9 Caring Leaders are Change-Oriented

They affect the course of history, the strata of society, and the state of mind. "But how is this all done?" you may ask. The mapping concept will help illustrate how caring leaders influence others. What we call a map is only a calibration of points well marked. Maps give direction. But notice two words here: *point* and *mark*. A distance comprises two or more points. Each distance leads to a definite mark, what we call a destination.

A mark is thus made by mapping points. It's like the writing of a good thesis. Points will make the whole. So it is in life. You leave a mark from each and every point you make on the way to your destination. The things you do every day add up to what your resultant mark will be. Every act, deed, or word you say is a point towards the mark you are trying to leave. And caring leaders make points in people's lives, one on one, and as a community of people. True influence begins when you make a point in someone's life, which eventually leads to a mark on life.

#10 Caring Leaders are Disciplined

They are sticklers to matters of character and morality. Caring leaders are a role model to the younger and upcoming generation. And what could be a better gift to leave to posterity than the gift of a caring heart? Because of their outstanding character and integrity of life, caring leaders are able to inspire the young to live meaningful and upright lives. They are very instrumental in instilling virtuous principles in their followers. As a result, the young can obey laws and contribute their talents, ideas, abilities, and etcetera, to the entire social fabric.

Caring leaders live above blame. They are a good source of mental power and excellent moral caliber. Leaders who don't care for the future are not worth the salt. But a future-minded leadership cares how posterity will survive. And the best way to protect the future is to invest in the moral development of the youth. When they learn from their leaders how to be morally upright they will not throw delinquent histrionics on society nor flout established social mores.

Being Your Brother's Keeper

The story of Abel and his brother Cain in the Bible is often quoted as an example of care negligence or even as a bad example of care. Cain didn't care at all for his brother. In fact, he murdered him. This story, however, brings us two points. The first one is that lack of care leads to death. This can be the death of potential, gift, or resolve. When you neglect to care, you are helping the quick demise of the thing or person you neglect to care for. When you care you are giving life. Do you get the point? We call those who kill people, murderers. What about those who kill dreams and aspirations?

Secondly, we are urged to be our brother's keeper. When you get into the subway, everyone you see becomes your brother or sister. Wherever you are and whomsoever you meet, that is your brother or sister. When they are in trouble, do not ignore them—help them. Rise to the occasion. Be your brother's keeper. We all love the security of our own immediate families. We work hard and invest in their lives. We take them to caregivers and we value their dreams and goals. What we do for our own families, we should also do for others.

People, unfortunately, take this mentality of not caring even to public offices. If you don't have a concept of caring, I am afraid even if they offer you a huge office it would not do. As they say, "Charity begins at home." Caring well for your family does not mean you know how to care. You know how to care when you understand that the same intensity with which you care for members of your closest family is required to care for others.

People Who Care are Fair

The essence of caring lies in the truth that everyone, regardless of race, background, age, gender, nationality, color of skin, education, status in life, sex-orientation, skill, etcetera, is important and deserving of your attention and care. That's when you begin to live life to the fullest.

When you discriminate and draw boundaries of apartheid, racism, bigotry, prejudice, intolerance, bias, or chauvinism, you become narrow-minded and incapable of being a true human leader. Caring is the basis for humanity and the flame that keeps human life alive.

IV

THE NATURAL LAW OF SEASONS

11

WHIZ WINTER'S WAVES

Knowing how to deal with adversity is one of the most decorated symbols of leadership.
— Charles Mwewa

There is a natural law of seasons which states that there is a time for everything. There is a time for joy as well as a time for sadness, and time for planning as well as time for executing the plan. The secret is that everything is made beautiful in its own time. When you observe seasons, you will notice that they are structured. Each season comes at a certain time of the year and seasons are mutually exclusive. They occur in tandem. And they are predictable. It is this concept of predictability that ensures survival.

Careful analysis of seasons will reveal that they rhyme with natural happenings as well as human experiences. Seasons define how the four elements of nature interact. Thus Winter, Spring, Summer, and Fall are consistent with snow, water, fire or light, and air or wind. These, in turn, coincide with the four tastes of life: bitterness, sourness, sweetness, and saltiness. It is the way these elements network that ensures natural balance and success.

Our experiences are also patterned on seasons. Thus there is a time of sadness, of hilarity, of joy, and of despair. All these experiences bring harmony and balance to human nature. Seasons teach us two lessons about success: *preparation* and *opportunity*. The question is not: will seasons change? But rather: are we prepared for season changes? And the catch is: how do we make use of seasonal changes? What opportunities in time are there for us to explore?

In life, it is not about what happens, so much as how you respond to what happens that matters. Success is not linear, and neither is influence. It is through the ups and downs, the mountains and valleys of life that you find a middle line for success. The Natural Law of Seasons helps us to maintain our composure and face the challenges of life with confidence. It also helps us to be ready for any circumstance, and to seek for opportunity in every adversity.

Inherent Opportunities in Adversity

Knowing how to deal with adversity is one of the most decorated symbols of leadership. Most successful leaders have had to overcome numerous forces working against them. They have to deal with loneliness, fake friends, stress, and unexpected enemies. In fact, true leadership has a lot to do with problem solving and averting adversity. Situations and circumstances will emerge to derail your drive and hinder progress.

The biggest mistake most people make is to focus entirely on the problem and lose sight of the promise of a solution. Leaders in particular should understand that trouble is unavoidable and even attractive sometimes. When you successfully overcome adversity, you gain valuable experience about what to do in case of a similar situation. The rule of thumb is not to quit, no matter what hardship you are facing.

Quitters Don't Win

It is often said that quitters are losers. Too many people quit just when they are about to hit the trophy of their lifetime. It's as if you were digging for gold. Each small hit you make contributes to the larger whole. The good news is, you are almost hitting gold, but the bad news is, you are not told.

So, keep striking, because you do not know which blow will break the crust. You may be attempting to achieve something in life but find yourself inhibited. Don't quit. Try again. So long as there is breath in you, that long you should persist. For then you will know one of the greatest principles of success — that if you persist long enough you will win.

Keep doing the same thing again and again until you get a breakthrough. There is chance for everyone who attempts. There is nothing for anyone who does not try! Risk takers are history makers. Risk taking is responsibility. Question the process, and challenge how things are done. Know that in every adversity there is provided for you an opportunity to succeed.

When everything seems to be blurred, keep your head above the water. That's how you overcome the storm gulp. Always observe the silver lining. That's how you reach the top. When there is nowhere to look, summon your inner resolve. That's how you keep the hope. And fight your battles with the end in mind.

You may gain some inspiration from Nelson Mandela. Even when he was in the grimmest of times in prison, and when with his comrades they were pushed to their limits, he would see a glimmer of humanity in one of the guards. That was enough to reassure him to keep on going. Like Nelson Mandela, often the people who influenced the world had to overcome much opposition and adversity to better theirs and other people's lives. Sorrow indeed may endure for the night, but joy shows up in the morning!

The Law of Seedtime

Harvest time is the most important time in a farmer's life. It is during this time that the farmer realizes his or her potential. All the times of hard work and sleeplessness come to be rewarded with a bountiful harvest. Now the farmer can enjoy his labor and meet various needs. But before this happens, a farmer has to plant the seed. Seedtime is crucial to a good harvest. If the farmer plants choice and healthy seeds, he is guaranteed a good harvest. If, on the other hand, he is careless in selecting his seeds, there will be nothing to look for during harvest.

How you live your life, and the impact you leave behind you, depends to the larger extent on the law of seedtime and the law of harvest. The law of harvest states that you reap more than you sow. When you sow a good thought, you will reap a kind word. Sow an altruistic act, and you will reap unselfish love. Sow a progressive habit, and you will reap in kind and deed. And when you sow in good character, you will reap a greater destiny.

Every day we live we are selecting and planting our seeds. If we plant seeds of love and goodwill, we will reap a harvest of peace and benevolence. If we are careless in our seed selection, we may reap a bogus harvest. Influence happens in stages. People are not affected overnight. As we do good deeds, we are steadily planting seeds of greatness.

In the 1990s I had a good share of motivational speaking engagements. I spoke in churches, in schools, in open rallies, as well as to corporate audiences. My theme was simple: motivate, motivate,

motivate! Whether it was to inspire confidence, to encourage progress, or to urge people not to give up on their dreams, my resolve and enthusiasm were always the same.

During this period I began helping an Asian lady who was suffering from depression. It took nearly two years of repeated counseling before she could heal totally. During this time of depression her relations with people were in pretty bad shape, her health was deteriorating, and she had developed two severe phobias, towards flight and swimming. In fact, she could not bath in her own bathtub!

Six years later this woman stood in front of over five thousand people to give a testimony. Little did I know it would center on me! I had long forgotten about her and the help I had rendered to her in the past. At that time, I believed I was merely doing what I loved doing, which is helping people succeed.

Her testimony brought tremendous attention to the nature of my ministry and added valuable credibility to my efforts. The seeds I had planted in that woman's life had bloomed into a bountiful harvest. In fact, she would later pay for my daily upkeep for nine consecutive months in my sophomore year at the university. People will not forget the deeds of charity and the contributions you make to their lives.

Mistakes Can Be Valuable Lessons

When people win a lottery or get promoted they usually open huge bank accounts to hoard their money. But what happens when you make a mistake? Do you curse yourself, or do you look for the seed of truth in it? Here is what you should do when you make a mistake. See if there is any valuable lesson you can learn from it, and then store it in the bank of your heart. Remember to do this because you will need this lesson in future.

Most people are too hard on themselves, especially when they make mistakes. It's like a part of them has been amputated. They fall into a quandary of despair and a quagmire of disrepair. What they don't know is that some mistakes can be valuable experiences worth noting. Not all the mistakes you make are wasters—some are future assets.

The Oxford English Dictionary defines a mistake as an error of judgment. In literary criticism that spells tragedy. Like most people, for a long time I also thought it was tragic to make mistakes. I believed that you had to be concise, precise, and accurate, always. But I was wrong. Most success stories have been written from the note pads of error. Here are three facts about mistakes:

Firstly, a mistake is the shortest route to goal achievement. Think about this. You want to reach a particular goal. You want to make sure you arrive there in comfort while accomplishing greatly. Chances are that you might want to take your time and be as cautious as possible. The reality is that you might just waste your time, and that is not a good thing. Nevertheless, there is a shorter way to goal achievement. Basically be willing to make mistakes.

Secondly, through a mistake, you may discover the way in which some things don't work. A mistake can be the greatest teacher when you look for signs of opportunities in it. When you conceive an idea, don't be afraid to try it. Understand that great ideas only become great realities because someone is willing to make mistakes. Because once you make a mistake, you've learned what doesn't work!

Thirdly, future victories are often born from past mistakes. It's often difficult to find a successful leader or businessman who did not make at least one serious mistake in his or her career. Good leaders learn from past mistakes. Successes are rarely good teachers; mistakes are. People generally gain new insights and perspectives about themselves by reflecting on what they did wrong and how they can do better in future. It is one of the secrets of success to refuse to let temporary setbacks defeat you.

Bank of Past Glory

In North America, success in securing employment or access to the status bar hinges on experience. If you come from Africa, or some selected European nations, one of the things that greets you is, "Hallow, welcome to America, kindly show us what you can do, but know that we only accept Canadian or US experience!" Then it dons on your mind that all your experience from elsewhere is of little use here. No wander it is not uncommon in North America to find foreign-educated degree holders driving taxis or forklifts in factories!

One day I was busy shopping at a Metro store. My car had a little mechanical problem, so I opted for a cab. Taxi drivers, by virtue of their job, are courteous individuals. This guy introduced himself as an immigrant from Ethiopia. He then told me that he was a medical doctor back home, and the system has made it hard to practice medicine in Canada. So he resorted to taxi-driving in order to fend for his family.

I had befriended another guy at a coil mattress factory I worked in Toronto. In Africa, his government had sponsored him to study as a mechanics engineer in Russia. Since arriving in Canada he had not been allowed to work in his field of training. He was, in fact, told to use his credentials to vie for a technician position.

At first I thought the system was unfair. But after some time I began to understand. In Canada, as in the United States, experience is everything. The North American culture teaches that there is value in past experience. North Americans would rather entrust their lives into the hands of an experienced nurse than risk with an inexperienced valedictorian doctor. It just makes sense.

I am an ardent soccer fan. I am enchanted by the English Premier League, the Spanish Ole la Liga, the Italian Serie A, the German Bundesliga, the French First League, the US-Canada Major Soccer League, the Central-Southern Africa COSAFA, and so on.

The game of soccer honors past glory. A team that has won the league or a player who has scored more goals in the past retains the visage of prestige and prominence among the rest. You must understand that in professional soccer that means the difference between thousands and millions of dollars!

The same thing happens in boxing. Here too, experience pays. Whether it is through the tale of the tape or the rituals that precede the fight, one boxer will be intimidated by another, for sure. In the 2000 boxing history the bout between the "Pretty Boy" Floyd Mayweather, Jr. and one "Golden Boy" Oscar De La Hoya attracted tremendous media attention.

Despite his renown and talent, De La Hoya was defeated even before the bout. Mayweather had won the fight outside the ring. Reason? Experience—not only with the power punch, but with his rhetoric as well. Floyd had learned from experience that you can overawe your opponent with words. And it worked for him. The legendary Mohammed Ali was also known to talk his way from one victory to another. In December 2007, Mayweather would go on to win the bout against the undefeated "Hit Man of Manchester" Ricky Hatton through a check-hook knock-out! And in 2014, he remained undefeated in 47 bouts. At his best, Mayweather was undefeatable, partly because of his skill-set and also because he sold himself well.

In church they have a song called "Count Your Blessings, Name Them One by One." Why do the rich nations insist on experience, or sports heroes master the gimmick of manipulating past glory? For one thing, it works, for another, by counting your past blessings, you re-energize yourself to go just another mile. You position yourself to face yet another challenge. As a matter of fact, your past glory may be your key to future trophies!

Do not underestimate the power of past contributions. Everything you do for humanity, or for yourself, clearly defines your intentions. It gives you an entrance into the annals of greatness. Sometimes you might feel as though you are overtly promoting yourself. But the fact of the matter is, the richer the bank of your past glories, the more secure your present investments.

The Crippling Nature of Excuses

For a long time I have had a very good habit. If you came to me with an excuse, I would look you straight in the eye and ask you to face your demons squarely. I developed this habit after I observed that people generally love to practice self-pity. Given an occasion, everyone is capable of a long narration about what they believe is not working too well in their lives. Most people love to give the impression that things are not right in their lives. They think that by giving such excuses they will make people sympathize with them.

Usually, people blame others when things are not happening according to their expectations. They look for possible outlets, people and events they can blame for their state of affairs. The difference between champions and failures is the way they handle excuses. Most people would simply freak out and lose the opportunity to confront their nemeses. In life you don't win or influence others by laying excuses, blames, or faults. You win by facing up to your challenges. You learn to achieve in life.

People have everything within themselves to succeed. A baby comes with nothing, and yet gains everything within minutes of being on earth. It even knows how to demand for more.

Indeed, human beings are born to achieve. They are born to be more than just naked flesh with blood. They are born to attain to greatness, to increase and to prosper.

Think you can, and allow yourself to.

People are born to achieve in three areas: in material things, in their intellect, as well as spiritually. Materially, people are born to acquire property such as lands, chattels, and personal effects like clothes. They can also acquire luxuries, money and basic needs like food, shelter and sex. Material advancement also includes access to good health, personal hygiene, attractiveness and to being presentable.

People are born to achieve intellectually. They are entitled to be accepted in society, to academic advancement, and leadership excellence. They can also attain intellectually in terms of good paying jobs, power and influence, as well as happiness and self-actualization. The first step towards being a champion is to believe in yourself before others do.

Spiritually, people strive to achieve a state of peace and tranquility within, as well as peace with other people. They also want to achieve personal wholeness and favor with fellow human beings and with God. Of the three areas, the greatest is spiritual although I placed it third.

You can achieve greatly in any or all of these areas. No-one was born with a mission statement or a bill of achievement. People learn to achieve. Achievement with contentment is of great reward. Achievement must be tempered with wisdom; for we will all leave behind whatever we achieved. Therefore, the best attitude for achievement is to do it in such a way as to bless God and others, and to reckon each achievement as a gift from above.

If things are not happening according to your expectations, try to pray.

12

SPRING TOWARDS THE SKY

The easiest way you can know whether
you have self-respect or not is in the way
you view and treat other people.
— Charles Mwewa

Society puts a premium on our compliance to certain moral standards. These standards are partly reinforced by the enactment of certain laws which restrict our behavior. But there is no nobler task than that of self-respect. People can lose their language and still discover they have plenty of opportunities to reacquire another. There are all kinds of insurances to life, chattels, and intellectual property. But there is none for the loss of self-respect. Self-respect is one of the grandest prerogatives of human capacity. To guard your sense of self-respect is to protect one of your life's greatest human endowments. In leadership, self-respect is not only highly regarded, but is also endorsed by some sort of policy, because a person who has lost self-respect cannot respect the property and the life of another.

The Centrality of Self-Respect

The easiest way you can know whether you have self-respect or not is in the way you view and treat other people. How do you see other people, people who are different in some way from you, for instance? Do you see them as inferior or creepy? How about your subordinates: are they human or simply means of production? Certainly your view of others is the clearest reflection of yourself. If you believe that other human beings are important and valuable, it is evidence of your own self-respect.

People who influence their world and change society for better are men and women who value their own self. They can change others because they have the power to change themselves. The power to change is the intrinsic capacity leaders have. Whenever it is appropriate, change is a positive thing. Resisting change can be detrimental to progress at any level. And leaders who have self-respect do contemplate change if such a change can improve them to lead better.

Fear is Not Free

One of the reasons most people dislike change is due to fear of the unknown. Whether you are a leader or not, learning how to deal with fear is a must-possess ability. It takes faith to move from point A to point B. To make profit in business takes some form of risk. To lead people takes confidence. To begin a project takes a lot of foresight. Fear is the number-one enemy of faith. It comes to frustrate your sense of risk-taking. And fear endangers progress in your life by inhibiting your confidence. When you submit to fear, you close tight all the doors of viable improvement.

Fear is one of life's greatest problems to overcome. Fear is costly. Fear will cost you money, relationships, promotion, opportunities to improve yourself, and so much more. For one thing, some people have gone to their graves with ideas that were never translated into reality; for another, those still alive live far below their capacity due to fear. Fear robs you. Fear victimizes you. It limits your chances to succeed and pours scorn on your talents and capabilities. There are so many people struggling to make ends meet while they have great talents. They will never allow their potential to emerge, due to fear. Each time they want to rise, fear brings them right down.

Fear forces you to procrastinate. You keep postponing action. You keep putting away today's actions for tomorrow. There are things that must come first in life. Certain actions are supposed to occupy a particular quadrant for certain results to come through. Some things are urgent; others are important. Some things are both urgent and important. Some actions need to be done today; doing them tomorrow may not yield the same results.

Are you in the habit of postponing action due to fear? Are you unable to perform today's job today? Are you a victim of procrastination? Perhaps the results you've always been wanting to have, have always been there but you've been a bit too preoccupied with the trivial and irrelevant. Do today's activities today, and achieve tomorrow's results tomorrow! Let first things come first!

Fear has so many bad effects. One of the commonest manifestations of fear is the fear to fail. Most people would have changed their situations had it not been for fear of failure. Most people would have improved the quality of their lives much more, but have been unable to do so because of the fear to fail. The fear of failure is failure itself. When you try something, you are already fifty percent likely to succeed. But if you fear to attempt, you have nothing to show for it, in any case. Some people fear to do certain things because they fear to be ridiculed if they should fail. But ask yourself, "What if I succeed?" It is better to attempt and fail, rather than fear to try anything.

Leaders especially must guard against the fear to attempt something big for their organizations. Even when they fail, they have in some way succeeded because they have learned valuable lessons from their experiences. Before I became a leader I thought that great leaders never failed. I thought that they were great because they always succeeded. But I was wrong. I began to realize that you are not a great leader because you succeed, but because you've learned how to recover from failure.

Most people fail once and are finished. They become bitter. They become vengeful. They heap blame upon those they considered to have caused the failure. This is a losing attitude. A winning attitude recognizes the fact that there is failure, but then disregards the fact. True leaders persevere until they win. They consider every failure as a lesson in the school of success. Failure is not in falling, but in failing to rise up after a fall!

Failure brings two benefits to us: experience and opportunity. Experience, in the form of the knowledge, skill, know-how, and familiarity we accumulate as a result. Failure brings us a wealth of experience; we learn how things should not be done the next time! This may take time, but most people will only see the difficulties of the moment and even get discouraged. Leaders endure even in the midst of seeming impossibilities.

The opportunity that failure brings is a subtle one. The moment you fail, you begin to look to the next chance. You become open-minded to possibilities. Success usually tends to make us contented. But you must understand that success is a process. And failure should not be seen as the end

of that process. Failure should be looked at
as a vital link in the success chain. Victory
comes with making adjustments after each
failed attempt, until the desired result is
achieved.

Failing once or twice is nothing.
Personally, I fail so many times before I
finally hit the gold. Sometimes I attempt
only once and succeed; but many a time
success comes after numerous attempts.
The Bible says that a man can fail seven
times and still rise again. I may not know
what kinds of challenges you're facing right
now. But keep moving, anyway. Because
you know that failing is an integral part of
life, especially when you constantly strive to
learn, grow, and stretch for new levels of
success!

People who enjoy success and influence
are also people who have known how to
recover from failure. In all my life I have yet
to come across a man or woman who would
claim not to have failed in life even once.
Libraries and museums are full of stories of
the brave and the celebrated. They are
brave and celebrated because they had to
endure numerous trials and challenges to
achieve something great. They failed; but
they never gave up. They saw the glories of

the victories ahead of them as having greater value than their prevailing circumstances. You can only be among that number if you don't give up on your dreams, even though there may be obstacles in the way. When you take a risk, you are making history.

The Gift of Youth

It is said that the pride of youth is in their strength, while the glory of the old is in their grey hair. Dreams in life are very important. We should not fear to dream. Most of our dreams come in our youth, which makes it the most productive age of life. Everyone who is a grownup now has been a youth before. There are only three kinds of people who have not yet tasted youth: the unborn, the stillborn, and those still in childhood. Otherwise, all of us have been endowed with the world's greatest natural resource, that of youth. Youth represents two great traits: strength and vision.

Youth is the hub of strength and energy. Physical strength is of great value to human survival. It brings tremendous benefits. A sound body and energized physique will help the youth do what most adults will struggle to do. As you grow older, you begin to see the difference between speed in youth and laxity in adulthood. Most people agree that the youth stage is the best age to invest one's life in.

This age is filled with excitement and vitality. A young person can easily move from place to place and handle weights that would be impossible for an older adult to handle. He or she has the added advantage of enjoying most activities the elderly will find not exciting. It is in youth that you lay the best foundations for a life of wealth and prosperity.

Youth is not only viable for physical strength; research has proven that the youth stage is endowed with mental agility as well. We are more mentally alert and dexterous in our youth stage than in adult years. Our brains naturally begin to slow down at the young age of thirty. Despite the fact that we can easily revitalize the brain "hardware" through habits like exercise, resting, eating healthy foods, and making relationships, our youth remains the most potent reservoir of our mental capacity. At this stage our memory is strong, our resolve is solid, and our cognition is viable. We can therefore do more with our youth than with any age facility.

Let the old dream dreams and the young have visions. Characteristically, young people are capable, not only of envisioning, but also of bringing those visions to pass. I believe that visions are the prerogative of youth because they have the excitement and the drive to move forward. A vision, discussed at length in Chapter Twenty, is a mental picture of a desired future. In your youth you are more interested in your future than in anything else. While old people are busy ruminating over past glories, the young are actively chatting a way forward to an illustrious future. Envisioning is the most superlative success attribute of youth.

If you are a young person, you should be actively involved with envisioning your future. You should not wait for older people to tell you to. Don't be like some people, who come to realize that they have not maximized their youth. Losing your youth can be the most disheartening experience of your lifetime. Plant seeds of greatness in your youth, and patiently wait for them to germinate.

If you do this, you will be glad when you reach the age of reckoning, an age when your physique and mental agility give up. At that time, you will wish you were a youth. The biggest upset of human experience is to wake up one day and find out that you are not a youth anymore. And the bad news is you never made the best use of your youth. Whatever you do, do not misuse your youth—the consequences are intractable.

13

SING SUMMER'S SURGES

> Love is the highest characteristic of
> human leadership.
> — *Charles Mwewa*

There is a striking relationship between leadership and love. Love impacts leadership in the same way the sun impacts the earth. The sun gives heat and light to the inhabitants of the earth. It also gives enhanced life to both fauna and flora through photosynthetic processes. So is love to leadership. It brings life, warmth and brightness to the leadership experience. I have defined leadership here as the art of loving people and spending yourself for them. There is no greater task on earth than that of leading people. In any industry, people are the greatest asset. Leading them is a privilege, not a right.

The Most Excellent Way

If you are going to leave a lasting impact on the people you lead, you must love them first, and then lead them. No other motive should propel you into leadership, apart from that of a genuine concern for them and their good. Those who think that leadership is a springboard to power or wealth are mistaken. When the former is the motive, disillusionment and frustration will be the outcome. Selfishness should not be the motive for leading people, either. In business management, leadership is a key requirement for managers. Leaders are carefully chosen, so that they can influence individuals and groups to cooperatively achieve organizational goals.

The love factor is an important aspect of leadership because leaders need to have excellent human relation skills. A leader's influence should create an enjoyable and productive atmosphere for everyone. Under a great leader, people want to work together to get the job done. Under threat and a negative environment, people may obey a bad leader and even get the job done. But in the long run, they will not work as effectively and efficiently as they should.

Followers look for leaders with a human face, leaders who can communicate information and give direction in a loving manner. As much as they know that a leader should be able to solve problems and make decisions, people also understand that a good leader must have their interest at heart. He or she must recognize their unique qualities and positively exploit these differences in his or her quest to bring the organization closer to attaining its goals.

Love is the highest characteristic of human leadership. Among others are understanding, confidence, objectivity, and good judgment. Some leaders are born; others are developed. But whatever the case, leaders should learn to be dependable, decision-oriented, and innovative. They should allow their leadership styles to harmonize with the wishes and aspirations of the people. Traditionally, leadership has been regarded as a set of rigid rules that impede the followers' responsiveness. This has led to leadership being viewed entirely as masculine, with no heart for pliability.

Leadership styles are generally seen as falling into four categories: autocratic, democratic, open, and servant-leadership. Effective leaders are those who consider a particular situation before deciding on their leadership style. Some people have called them Situational Leaders because they take into account the personality of their followers, along with the particular task at hand, before deciding which style will be most appropriate.

The Art of Loving People

The best style of leadership is servant-leadership. Servant-leadership fosters a spirit of selflessness in meeting the needs of the people. Servant leaders go out of their way to serve those they lead. Their joy comes from serving the people. They work hard, and invest themselves in the people, and derive great satisfaction when those they lead succeed. They can do all this because they lead by love.

The Toronto Police's maxim reads: "To Serve and Protect." That is what love does: it serves others and protects. Love does not boss others around, because love considers serving others as a great duty to humanity. It makes the earth a lovely place to live in. Serving others is a virtue that is impeccably humane, faultless, and flawless! Love looks for opportunities to serve others.

Too many people want to know how they can serve their world. My advice: begin where you are, with what you have. Serve with your time, resources, finances, talents, abilities, graces, position, and so on. Usually, love doesn't need money—just a word of comfort, an act of kindness, or a philanthropic deed can do. Most altruistic individuals are usually simple people with no great financial muscles. They simply give of themselves. They are selfless and unselfish. They go out of their way to improve other people's lives and therein make a difference.

To whomsoever you direct your love, there your greatness is. This principle helps leaders channel their useful energy in safeguarding the interests of the people. Your greatness is neither in the monuments you have built nor in the memorabilia you have accumulated through the years. Your greatness is in the selfless sacrifices you make for the people. If you want to leave a lasting legacy, invest yourself in the people. Help them reach their greatness, and you will reach yours. Give them wings to fly, and they will carry you up and high.

There is little love in what you say; much love is in what you do. Words are powerful.

Words can change things. But when it comes to true leadership, deeds speak louder than words. You can say all you want, but it's what you do that justifies or denigrates you. It is what you do, not what you say, that will meet people's needs!

A Place of Influence

The most important place to exert influence is where you are. Whether you are a housewife, a student, a professional, or a parent, the people you immediately interact with are your primary source to influence. Begin where you are, with the people around you. Influence them by love. Show it through your actions, behavior, and attitudes. Model love before them in what you say and do. And motivate them by love because love is the greatest motivational force.

Love is the ability to respond to challenges. A president of a country loves his nation when he leads the people well in difficulty times. A parent loves her children when she brings them up in dignity and discipline. A teacher loves her students if she teaches them the basic principles of success and imparts them for the future. A couple loves itself when it averts a divorce and stays on course. And the list goes on and on.

When you take on leadership, you are courting with responsibility. You've learned to care for those you love. And by taking responsibility, you are truly influencing people towards self-sufficiency. You may be wondering what responsibility is. In a nutshell: responsibility is duty and dependability. Duty to country, to family, to the organization, or to a nobler cause, is a principal leadership calling. But leaders should also be dependable. Those who are led should be able to count on their leaders.

Endangered Species

Grace was one of the discussants on the digital forum on my website where we mulled over issues of general concern. She once wrote expressing her disappointment over leaders who demand to be paid before they help people. These leaders, she said, wanted to be compensated for their insights and speeches. They fixed higher prices on what they offered. And she wondered why these leaders insisted on being remunerated if their motive was to help people.

Let's face it, the current view of assistance is pay half, get the rest. Profit and gain run our world. No one seems to care anymore whether someone is helped or not. We can safely say that we now live under the dispensation of greed. They say that one man's trash is another man's treasure. When that saying is applied to the human condition, nothing but travesty is expected. Human beings are priceless. And human beings deserve selfless and dedicated men and women to lead them.

What Grace was concerned about was the scarcity of dedicated leaders—who lead for the love of leadership! There is nothing in this world as disheartening as doing something that you don't love, and doing it day after day. It's one thing to have followers or employees who show up to work even if they don't like what they do. But it is another thing to have a leader who hates his job. It is surely an accident waiting to happen.

If you hate your job, and you are a leader, resign before you plunge the company into hell loop. A leader must be dedicated to his work. Leaders who have influenced their world are and were those who loved what they did. They gave of themselves in what they did. They went miles and miles of sheer service and dedication. They were not interested in their position only, but in what they could do to help those they led. They are and were selfless servant-leaders.

Are you a leader? Do you have a position of influence where you direct and command some authority of some sort? It does not matter how insignificant your leadership assignment is. What matters is the size of your dedication in your leadership role. When you are dedicated to your leadership duties you attract others who will help you achieve greatly. Dedicated leaders are few and in short supply. Yet they are necessary because they make a difference to their world in a meaningful way.

Still, anyone can be a dedicated and selfless leader. All it takes is love. Love the people you lead and the cause for which you lead them. Let every moment count. Give people the reason to exist. Inspire them to reach and achieve their dreams. Be a model of confidence in what you say and do. Rise to the challenge when none is willing. And always lead your people by example. Because you have the most impact on people who perceive that their leader or leaders love what they do.

Yes, You Can

Most people would have been very successful had it not been for their own mouths. By what they say, they have already counted themselves out from the potential prize. People who rarely succeed are those who are negative and critical. They see impossibilities and difficulties in everything. And most of all, they say it. Some people erroneously believe that by confessing negatively they will achieve positive results. Life is not like that. You get what you order. And you tend to become what you constantly affirm.

You can be what you believe to be. You can do what you believe you can. It is as simple as that. How do you think other people did it? They only believed. They are not superheroes; superheroes are only found in fiction books and movies. In real life there are real people, facing real-life challenges. The rich are rich because they do certain things that make them rich. Those who are powerful are so because they do and say powerful things. What about those who are nothing? They may be so because they do and say nothing.

One friend of mine told me, "I have done everything, Charles, and nothing seem to be happening." I don't believe in such sentiments. Anyone who does something will achieve something. That's just how nature fixed its rules. If you take a stationary stone and throw it in the air, it will come back. If you keep it where it is, that is, if you do nothing, it will remain where it is.

Similarly, if you do nothing about your situation, it will not change. Know that you will get run over if you just sit there, even if you are on the right track. Doing nothing is the greatest self-induced injustice. But saying you can't is the worst self-inflicted punishment you can ever experience. When you say that you can't, you limit your own potential. But when you say you can, you open doors to infinite possibilities. Everyone who has done or achieved something worthwhile believed that they could. They encountered impediments and obstacles, but still believed regardless.

Martin Luther King Jr. believed he could change the culture of racial discrimination in the United States of America. When he declared in that famous speech, "I have a dream," he was merely regurgitating what was true inside of him. Nelson Madiba Mandela believed he could upset the apartheid system of South Africa when he went to prison for twenty-seven long years. Walt Disney believed he could make people happy when he began the Walt Disney World. President Barack Obama believed he would become the first African-American president of the United States of America. When he spoke those three most powerful words, "Yes, We Can," he was only affirming what was true and noble in the inside of him.

Frank, the father of Belinda Stronach who was one of Canada's most influential female politicians, believed he could make it in the automotive industry. He found a job, got fired, saved enough money to take a bus to Kitchener, where he begged for a job that eventually gave him enough money to buy a tool kit to start his own company. Today he heads Magna International Inc., the multibillion-dollar automotive-parts company he founded.

What about everyday heroes like us who have to overcome various huddles to secure a good future for ourselves and our families? Think of countless others who believe they can. They are the ones running our governments, our department stores, our retail outlets, our banking facilities, our churches, and the list is endless. Because they said they could, they have made life easy for everyone. Today you can join that list, too. You can begin to believe that you can. You can resurrect that dream of yours that died because you thought only a few were destined to succeed. You can believe today by saying those important three words: "Yes, I can!"

Last Legacy

Some people are made by circumstances; others use circumstances to their advantage. We call the latter enthusiasts. There is nothing like the power of enthusiasm in the quest to bring a dream to pass. Enthusiasm wins the day, conquers limitations, and ignores dissuasions. Every time you begin to do or make something for yourself there will be others who will come to discourage you. They will look you in the face and tell you to stop. They will tabulate reasons why you will not succeed. They know people who attempted a similar mission and failed. They will provide evidence why it is foolhardy to go ahead and do what you want to do.

Enthusiasm is the passion to accomplish something. It will be seen in your actions, heard in your voice, and discerned in your spirit. Enthusiasm is the flame that lights up your path. It is the energy that keeps you moving. When you lose your enthusiasm, you lose the power to carry on. Anything can come to a standstill without it. Enthusiasm says "no" to the voice of discouragement. Enthusiasm says, "I will try; I will give it my best and see what happens." When you are enthusiastic about something you refuse to listen to the voice of reason, even though reason is important. You elect to listen to your heart. You are convinced that what you are doing is the right thing for you.

In leadership, enthusiasm is not only an asset, but it is also the engine that propels the leadership machine. An enthusiastic leader will inspire his or her people to carry on even when failure is staring them in the face. There are challenging times in leadership. There are times when morale is low and the levels of stress are high. There is no better time to display the virtue of enthusiasm than in these times. Enthusiasm is contagious; it will filter through to others and cause production or achievement to be possible.

I know you have a dream. I will only urge you to do one thing: be enthusiastic. Do not allow the challenges of the moment to derail your progress. Maybe you immigrated to another country, and you are jobless. You've tried to apply to several companies, and they keep turning you down. Maybe you were educated in another country, but here they can't accept your credentials. Maybe you are working under a boss you believe to have lower qualifications than yourself. Maybe you are on the verge of divorcing, or your partner is threatening an end to your relationship. May be you come from a country with limited possibilities for advancement. May be you desire to improve yourself but you are hampered by physical, social and personal handicaps. How do you survive these perilous states of affairs? The answer is enthusiasm. Keep your enthusiasm; and enthusiasm will see you through to the desired end.

If there is anything you wish to leave with your children, let it be enthusiasm. You may not attain greatness or be rich yourself. But let your children believe they can. Encourage their spirit through enthusiasm. Most people lose even before they begin. They are timid. They lack confidence. Enthusiasm is the matter champions are made of. You can achieve whatever you put your mind to through enthusiasm. Let not fear and cowardice militate against your progress. Be enthusiastic, and inspire others through your enthusiasm.

Even when you face challenging situations, maintain an enthusiastic pose. It is true that sometimes circumstances may not favor you. And there are times when you may feel like your world is tumbling down. Unfortunately, such days will be many in life. Sometimes, just when you think all is fine, trouble may be lurking around the corner. And in life you cannot be absolutely certain that money, fame, or success will bring you happiness. However, in any situation in which you may find yourself, it is important to maintain your own peace of mind. That's what enthusiastic people do; they keep their own peace of mind. A human system is like any other system, if a part of it is not performing well, that part affects the rest of the system. Trusting in something bigger than ourselves secures a peace of mind. Faith in God is always of great help in such situations.

Most Effective Sleeping Pill

In order to maintain a sustained level of peace of mind, the brawling menace of anxiety must be dealt with. Anxiety is the number-one enemy that robs you of peace of mind. It is the angst of mental instability, and it drives people to commit all kinds of regrettable acts.

Leaders ought to learn to sleep on peace of mind. There is no sleeping pill more effective than a rested mind. A mind in turmoil is a recipe for disaster. Jesus said: "Do not let your hearts be troubled." Troubled waters sink ships, but troubled minds sink dreams. You don't want to sail on raging waves. Look up, square your shoulders, and declare that the storm is over now. That's how champions win.

Qualms of Life

People often have qualms over three things: for their past, they regret; for their present, they are dumbfounded; and for their future, they jitter. Worry, like its cousin anxiety, is a crippling enemy. Worry lets you think so much and do so little. It wastes your time and sometimes, arising from this, makes what you are worried about come to pass. The danger is not in the fact, but in succumbing to the fact.

Worry is motivated by fear and a sense of insecurity. Worry is a time bomb, a detonator waiting to explode. Look at your life; how many of the things you've worried about have come to pass? The answer could be, little or none. But worry buffets you and causes headache in your mind. That's all that you gain by worrying.

One of the questions you have to answer about worry is: If you are not able to do the least, why are you anxious about the rest? People worry about food, clothing, and life. But who, by worrying, can add to his stature? In other words, why worry about the rest if you can't handle the least? We worry because we are constantly ignoring the large picture and only concentrating our efforts on the trivial. If we can't change the simple, why should we worry about what we can't fix?

The birds are so peaceful and it never even bothers them that they don't know where they will get their food. Flowers are beautiful, and yet they do nothing to maintain that beauty. If you are more important than birds and flowers, why do you worry about food and clothes? Once you understand this truth, you will not be perturbed anymore with feelings of worry.

Worry is painful. And the worse part about this pain is that it haunts the mind. "And do not seek what you should eat or what you should drink, nor have an anxious mind," says Jesus. Worry is a torture. It's a pain in the soul. Worry, by its nature, is foreign to the human body. It causes ulcers in the flesh. The more time you devote to worrying, the more damage it does to your bodily systems. People who worry too much have sleepless nights and unhappy lives. Whether you worry or not will not change what will happen. Wisdom is in *not* worrying, for doing so may enable you reach your goals with fewer side effects.

I have developed a habit of "sleeping on" very challenging issues. Sometimes when I receive bad news, I don't want to act immediately. Doing so might yield even worse results. So, I prefer to give it a moment and tackle it over the next day or days. In a state of worry even smart minds fail. The next time you are working on a complex problem, it will pay to sleep on it. A good night's rest will double your chances of finding a creative solution to your problems, whether they may be mathematics, LSAT, making administrative decisions, or just buying another car. Even scientists believe that a resting brain is capable of synthesizing complex information.

To Unknown Gods

The Greeks were zealous for new ideas, new inventions, and new philosophies. In Greek mythology certain gods were credited with creativity and mental agility. In ancient Athens there were even shrines dedicated to unknown gods. Athenians believed that these gods provided them with direction and guidance on the sea. It could have been Athena, Apollo, or Zeus himself, but whoever the god was, Athenians believed in him or her. This, in a sense, brought them tremendous peace of mind. Knowing that Apollo had sanctioned the voyage gave them complete confidence throughout the sea expedition.

It is believed that people who believe in a supreme being for guidance are much more stable and peaceful than those who trust in themselves alone. It pays to know that someone watches over you. It even pays more if that someone has power over you. Trusting in a higher power guards your mind and heart from anxiety. It is like a wall of protection against unwarranted thoughts. You don't need to embrace a particular religion to qualify for this kind of security. All you need is to believe that such power watches over you. A sense of peace and soundness is vital to living a purposeful and anxiety-free life.

People who have influenced their world believed in a power higher than themselves. They were motivated to pursue higher causes because of their trust in the higher power. This kind of inner contentment energized them to seek after lofty causes and to endure numerous trials to achieve their quests. In your own efforts, you may not do it, but with the help of the powers beyond yours, you can come face to face with destiny.

The greatest knowledge you can have is that of God. People who ignore the knowledge of God also ignore their own destiny. The knowledge of the Highest is the pathway to peace, the roadway to true riches, and the most infallible way to influence. With God on your side, you can call the impossible possible, and the impassable passable. With God, your view is clear, and your future is dear. Because when God is on your side, nothing can fall on your wayside.

For a long time people thought that religion was the opium of the poor. They believed that to be saintly was to abstain from the niceties of life and relegate intellectuality to oblivion. And yet Greece, the nation that has boasted of the brightest and greatest of world thinkers, was highly religious. Her men influenced the scholastic world and brought to civilization meritorious breakthroughs. And yet these same people sought after an unknown god! Religious piety is not in the homage paid to a particular deity, but in regarding your own life as a magnificent design of the master planner. You're not an accident, however many doubts you may have about yourself. God made you and he loves you.

14

FALL FROM FOLLY

God is an equalizer; he gave every one of
his creatures a brain.
— Charles Mwewa

Children grow up with a defensive mechanism called self-pity. It is necessary for children in childhood and adolescence to make it. Children need self-pity. They need it for their very own survival. When they are hurting, they look around, and one of the very few tools available to them is self-pity.

Self-Pity is a Problem

Self-pity brings mixed reactions to adults and toddlers alike. For adults self-pity may sometimes reduce their inner pain and put them to a comfortable rest. It may numb their discomfiture and bring a sense of temporary safety. Most people suffering from self-pity may not even acknowledge it. It is sort of a shield from intrusion into their privacy. It is this failure for most people to admit they have self-pity that makes self-pity one of the most addictive emotions of the human race.

Grownups should not tolerate self-pity. It's not an endearing experience or a soft emotion. In fact, it robs you of respect in the first place. Defined as the excessive concern with and unhappiness over your own troubles, self-pity paralyzes your thoughts, and feelings, and even your very actions in the world. Often, it becomes a pathetic manipulation that people use to get any number of things. At its worst self-pity may create a pitiful reality.

Self-pity is menacing both to you and society. That's the trouble with it. When you are swamped with self-pity you're actually leading a sorrowful life filled with problems and struggles. The lethal aspect of self-pity is the tendency to self-blame. I mean, when you come across people mired in self-pity, just observe how they blame everybody for their misery. No one is right. The government is bad. Neighbors are bad. No one is good at all. Self-pitiers erroneously believe that the source of their problems and struggle is outside of themselves.

The deception of self-pity is in the dilemma it creates for you—the failure to admit that you could be the source of your own problem. The thinking with self-pitying individuals is that someone or something else is the source of their problems. And when that happens, they are giving their power away to that something else. It's like saying that someone or something is more powerful than they are.

Self-pity does not positively change society. By its nature, self-pity does not and will not accept responsibility for its own fate. Someone else must be responsible. Victims of self-pity believe that another person, or the object of self-pity, must change in order for their lives to improve. In actual sense, what self-pity is doing to them is alienating them from themselves and others.

Self-pity is often in your own brain. So, although you may not know it at the beginning, you actually have the power to get rid of it. As I said earlier, you have to admit you are a victim of self-pity. This initial acceptance will lead you to hate the emotion and courageously embrace solutions that will alleviate the problem.

Most experts believe that you can bring self-pity under control by choosing a quiet place where you can picture your own self-pity. They advise to bring yourself to a concentration point in which you actually experience self-pity. In the intensity of the emotion, they implore you to imagine and visualize the self-pity soaring up and accumulating to a point where it overwhelms you. At that point, picture it as something terrible, which urgently needs to leave your life.

Freedom from self-pity will enable you to take responsibility for your own failure and success. As a leader you cannot thrust yourself in self-pity; it will rob you of the necessary element you need to command respect. People don't respect leaders, or anybody, for that matter, who feels that everyone around them is a problem. In political leadership, such leaders become dictators, because their self-pity drives them to the point where they feel insecure and incapable. The result is usually that they use the political machinery to eliminate and dispirit anybody whom they feel is responsible for their pitiable state of affairs.

Self-pity destroys relationships and impedes progress. A husband or wife who is a victim of self-pity will wrongly believe that his or her partner is the source of his or her problems. And the short cut is usually to seek divorce or separation. When that happens, the person may remarry, only to discover that the problems he or she thought had vanished are still prevalent. And this may lead to another divorce, becoming a vicious cycle. When you deal with your self-pity, you prevent yourself from many troubles.

More than a Computer

God is an equalizer; he gave every one of his creatures a brain. When you have the brain, what more can you ask for? The brain has been termed the world's greatest computer—and rightly so! I spend over forty percent of my free time on the computer. I don't claim omnipotence in the knowledge of the magic machine, even though I know it better than the average person, but I know something about it. I know that it can be made better, faster, and smarter. And so can the human brain.

How fast you solve problems, how smart you are at the game of life, or how much better you are in handling social or personal challenges depend in part on how good, fast, or smart your brain is. The good news is that you can improve your brain at any time. There are several things you can do. Traditionally, certain behaviors and practices have been known to increase the speed and aptitude of the brain. These include differential calculus, chess, mind games, and so on. But not everyone is a mathematician, or chess player, or mind-game enthusiast.

Research has found that the best way to keep your brain healthy and young is through aerobic exercise. Exercise increases the blood flow to the brain and decreases the risk of heart disease, diabetes, and obesity. Scientist have recently discovered that when you exercise, you enable the brain cells to release a chemical called the *brain-derived neurotrophic factor* (BDNF), which basically acts as a fertilizer for the brain. Isn't that amazing?

The other way in which we can improve our brains is through crossword puzzles, one of my favorite hobbies. I used to think that the brain deteriorates as we age. But science is refuting such hypotheses. It is now known that we actually grow new neurons, or brain cells. Studies show that if we are kept in an interesting environment, with lots to do and play, we can essentially grow more new cells. A friend of mine introduced me to a word-game, and I haven't been able to leave it alone ever since. And it is fascinating, too, to know that you can find things that interest you, because you can really get into them.

What about staying calm? Yes, studies again are showing that high levels of stress hormones have a negative impact on memory and learning in normal adults. One of the key ways of reducing stress is to identify the things that cause high blood pressure to soar and then to find the healthy way to relieve the stress. Apart from physical exercise, calmer activities, such as meditation, are great de-stressors.

Years ago, I read a small booklet written by Kenneth Haggins, Sr. Kenneth explored the idea of meditating prior to preaching. He discovered that he was more effective when he had spent quality time in calm meditation than when he spoke out his thoughts in prayer. I believe those moments of calmness propelled his brain to exponentially process his speech faculty, which in turn led to effective communication and idea synthesizing.

CHARLES MWEWA

When we concentrate our minds, we produce extra energy to help us deal with life's challenges. When we panic, we lose the tract necessary to think creatively and resolutely.

Circle of Friends

It is amazing how many people we meet every day. If you live in the Greater Toronto Area (GTA), you probably meet thousands of new faces each day. But have you ever asked yourself: "How many of these people do I actually know?" Candidly, maybe very few! Surprising, isn't it? But that's one of the ways in which our brain is deprived. Because courting a new friend is not only enjoyable but is also good for our minds.

Socializing is one of the best ways to brighten up the brain. Socializing seems to be as effective as more direct intellectual stimulation at exercising the brain, and may prevent the loss of mental function. How many friends have you made lately? You could be missing out on one of the world's most enjoyable forms of bettering the brain.

Thinker Mentality

It pays to use the brain. A few people who have used their brains productively have brought to the world massive revolutions in science, technology, the arts, media, politics, academia, and human development. Have you ever wondered what would happen if these kinds of men and women did not think? Consider the invention of the computer, the telephone, the airplane, and anything from the domestic flashlight to the industrial forklift.

One day I watched a documentary on television about a remote village in Venezuela. People who claim to be the real natives of Venezuela live in a very remote village, with no access to electricity and modern facilities. But they have devised creative means of preserving their food. What fascinated me, however, was how they have adapted to the marshy environment around them. In fact, they build their huts right over the swamp— creativity so rare, and yet so useful.

When people put their whole hearts to their brains they can come up with amazing ways of improving their own lives, and change society for good. You cannot change the world by simply watching; you do so by doing. When you engage your brain to productive potential you will be amazed how many ideas you can come up with. Ideas do not grow on trees. Ideas are the products of our minds. Virtually everything we see and use around us is someone else's idea that became a reality.

The trouble with most people is that they rarely make use of their ideas. It is said that the richest place on earth is not Fort Knox. The richest place on earth, rather, is the grave, for it is here that great ideas are buried, here where ideas lie that did not become realities. What sad a way to die! Society does not put limitations on how far or how great you can become. Society only responds to how much you allow it to limit you.

One of my friends transformed his love for communication into a force for social empowerment. What began only as an idea to motivate people had become a world-changing dream, culminating in a six-thousand dollar donation to the cause of Zambian education. Another friend of mine has used his Internet savvy to help create orphanages in Africa.

What idea do you entertain? What dreams do you have? You can influence your world only when you put your ideas to work for you. This book you are reading began as an idea. I was bored enough to refuse to listen to the voice of *what ifs* in order to spend time writing something you might be finding helpful right now. In other words, I translated my idea into a book. You can transform yours into anything you like.

The beauty of an idea is that, however insignificant and ridiculous you may think it is, there is someone out there who will find it helpful and interesting. Some people may find this book laborious and even boring. But there will be thousands who will think of it as a work of genius. So do not underestimate the power of an idea. It can come to be, but only when you put it to test.

Better Than First

You can read many books on leadership. You can hear speakers labor on this great subject. You will hear so many ideas of leading people and organizations. And one thing you will hear repeatedly is a trait all great leaders seem to possess: integrity.

History has a sharp-pointed pen. But history has also a sharp eraser. Most pages are opened in the annals of history, some stories that would have been great, sadly, are erased or scorned, all because of integrity. Integrity is the yardstick of leadership success. When all things are said and done, great leaders will be valued on their sense of integrity.

In the leadership race, the way you finish is more important than the way you began. In fact, most people are not even known when they begin. Right now, as you read this book, there are potential leaders in the making who you don't even have any idea exist. Some are being appointed to some new positions, and some are being promoted to more challenging situations. What you also don't know is how many of those countless leaders whom you don't know will make it into the halls of leadership fame.

What you do know are men and women who have made it through the ranks of leadership. Society can be blind to so many things. But one thing society has not done is fail to inform us about men and women who endured tests, narrowly escaped death, sacrificed all for the human cause, were imprisoned for standing up for the truth, dared not to give up hope when that hope meant the freedom of many people—and the list is endless. Most of these diligent men and women did what they had to do due to integrity. They went through what they had to go through because they had integrity. And they are read about, quoted in theses, and honored in word and deed, because they had integrity.

What then is integrity? I can answer this question by noting the different views associated with integrity. These views relate to the individual's character, social commitments, and personal virtue. The first of these views, the *self-integration* view of integrity, postulates integrity as a matter of a person integrating various parts of his or her personality into a harmonious, intact whole. In this aspect, integrity is primarily a matter of keeping the self-intact and uncorrupted.

A related approach to integrity is to think of it primarily in terms of a person's holding steadfastly true to his or her commitments, where *commitment* is seen as a general term covering many different kinds of intentions, promises, convictions, and relationships of trust and expectation.

The third view of integrity is the *identity* view. The identity view of integrity sees integrity largely as a personal virtue, a quality defined by a person's care of the self. In this regard, integrity manifests itself as a social virtue, one that is defined by a person's relations to others. Here, it is a person's proper regard for his or her own best judgment. Thus, men and women of integrity do not just act consistently with their endorsements; they stand for something worthwhile within a community of people.

A person of integrity cannot, therefore, be morally mistaken. Understood in this way, one only properly ascribes integrity to a person with whom one finds oneself completely in moral agreement. This concept of integrity does not, however, closely match ordinary use of the term. The point of attributing integrity to another is not to signal unambiguous moral agreement. It is often to ameliorate criticism of another's moral judgment. For example, we may disagree strongly with the prime minister's views of the role of women in law, take this to be a significant moral criticism of him, and yet admit that he is a man of integrity. In such a case, the point is largely to attribute integrity, to open a space for substantial moral disagreement without launching a wholesale attack upon another's moral character.

Integrity is a cluster concept, tying together different overlapping qualities of character under the one term. What is, consequently, central to integrity is that it is consistent with certain moral standards. I do not mean to suggest that a person of integrity must be affiliated with a particular religious belief system. A man or woman may not even belong to any particular religion, and yet he or she has integrity. Related to morality, integrity supposes that there are certain actions and behaviors that society has come to regard as moral. Honesty, truthfulness, faithfulness, and so on, could all be exemplary displays of integrity. In other words, integrity is the wholehearted pursuit of a peculiar moral end.

Integrity should not be confused with personal preferences and choices. Any person has a right to act or behave in any way so long as by doing so he does not break the law or infringe on another person's human rights. A person with integrity may display character traits and ways of behaving and thinking that tend to maintain the status quo. But at times, he or she may tend to act in ways that demand change.

One has to be careful to behave in a way that does not defeat integrity or an aspect of one's integrity. I have known great leaders who have divorced and still have integrity. I have also known men who have not divorced but who don't have integrity. So, whether one decides to stay with a marriage or abandon it is idiosyncratic to integrity. In one case, staying may indicate a lack of integrity, while in a different case, abandoning the marriage would indicate such a lack. It's up to an individual to judge which behavior or action displays integrity and which one does not.

To be a man or woman of integrity you don't need to be academically correct in your definition of integrity. As a matter of fact, you should not even bother to know or understand its derivatives. What you must know, nevertheless, are its properties. You will know someone has integrity when he or she acts honestly, truthfully, honorably, reliably, uprightly—and the list goes on.

To have greater social impact, you've got to strive to act or behave with integrity. I have noticed that people implicitly believe that integrity is the foremost leadership quality. Consider when people are bidding farewell to a leader. Whether it is at a company's farewell party, or a church's sending-away ceremony, someone will just not be able to forget about the integrity of the person in question.

A person being sent away might have accomplished greatly for the company or organization. He or she might have brought massive changes and colossal profits, and also by his efforts many great things might have happened. The people will remember all these. But they will tie them to how that person fared in the integrity department. We affect people not by what we did, but by how we did it. The only exception to this rule seems to be in science, and only to scientific inventions. The psychologist Carl Jung, credited as the father of analytical psychology, by his own admission, was not a complete man of integrity. But he has gone on to earn his respect by the monumental contributions he made to psychology.

I receive many emails from Africa, the United States, Canada, and Europe. People whose lives I have had an impact on at one time or another send me these emails. None, if any, of these people commend me for my skills or talents. But they all mention my sense of integrity. One young law student in Africa sent me an email detailing how even after six years in absentia, he was still inspired to extend up high by my principles and sense of integrity.

Another person from the United Kingdom reminded me how he has maintained a sober purpose-driven life, due to my influence on him in his earlier years. And I can recount hundreds of similar accolades. It all boils down to one thing—people rarely forget you when what you did or said to them, or for them, was done or said with an honesty attitude, to inspire them and bring out the best in them. They will even remember you more if your life matched your words!

Pruning Has Rewards

When a farmer perceives that a tree does not live up to its potential, he may prune it in order to allow it to produce more.

Pruning involves cutting off excess, but unproductive, branches from the tree. This usually results in growth and massive output.

The tree will grow more and better branches, bear more fruits, and remain healthy. Imagine now that the tree was a person. Cutting out human "branches" would prove to be a painful experience. But also imagine that, by doing so, such a person would become more efficient and effective! What's your guess? Pruning would be considered a necessary process.

In order for you to bear much fruit, some form of pruning is necessary. Leaders don't need to wait for someone to criticize or upbraid them; they should constantly be checking their own lives to ensure that they are living a life of integrity. When you take care of your own weaknesses and limitations, no one will point a finger at you. Self-discipline is a flawless antidote. If you wish to increase self-respect and integrity, learn to discipline and correct yourself. Prune yourself to fine-tune yourself. That's as easy as it gets.

V

THE GOLDEN RULE

15

GOLDEN-PLATINUM RULE

*What you do to others is what others will
do to you, only to you it will come in
increased measure; and as much as
possible, ask others how they would like
you to treat them.*
— *Charles Mwewa*

The Golden Rule is the Law of Love. No one in their right mind would like to do harm to themselves. This rule says, if you cannot harm yourself, so do not harm your neighbor either. In this rule you find the middle ground for confrontation. In other words, you play with the rules of compromise. Compromise is necessary to human relations. You can't do much without it. When you compromise for the sake of another, you love your neighbor as yourself.

Fair enough, let us consider that we all wanted to see positive results in everything we did. The next thing we would hope for is not to see someone else succeed ahead of us. We, as it were, die a little when a friend of ours succeeds. Not exactly a mindset that positively influences society. That's why we need the Golden Rule.

Keeping Up with the Joneses

Most people embrace unhelpful tendencies to measuring what they need by what other people have. The bottom-line is it is unwise to measure yourselves by yourselves and compare yourselves among yourselves. I have seen people who have stretched themselves beyond limits simply because they want to have what their neighbor has. It's a sort of "keeping up with the Joneses" or as it is in 2015, "keeping up with the Kardashians," kind of thing.

One thing we are learning, in a tough way, is that competition may bring us material goods, but it can't bring us peace. Our sense of self-worth keeps eroding away day by day, and we are slowly defining who we are in material terms. But with each passing day we are becoming more dissatisfied with everything we have achieved. We forget that true happiness happens when we put the interest of others ahead of our own. If we strive to bring happiness to others, others will go all-out to make us happy. This is based on what I call the Orbit Principle.

The Orbit Principle

The Orbit Principle is based on a very simple fact: whatever a person sows, that he or she will also reap. When you sow cone or maize, that's exactly what you are going to reap. Also known as the Principle of Input and Output, this principle postulates that whatever you put in is what you will get out. As in the practice of agriculture, the output always supersedes the input, all conditions accounted for. This means that what you do to others is what others will do to you; only to you it will come in increased measure.

We have for many years thought that this principle only applies to wrongdoing. We hear preachers warning: "Do not be deceived, God cannot be mocked; whatever a man sows that he shall also reap!" That is true according to biblical exegesis. But this principle is as true to right-doing.

Attracting people is like seed planting when we choose only our best seeds. Planting our best seeds might mean reaping a handsome harvest. If our lives where

179

guided by this rule, our actions would be done with caution. This principle hinges on specificity and affects the object very directly. All of our actions have consequences, some for good and others for bad. The good news is we can determine the outcome by what we choose to do.

You can choose to influence people positively with what you have, or say, or do; or you can elect to negatively influence people by the same. In essence, this principle postulates that you are responsible for what happens to you, if unforeseeable forces choose to be silent. Therein lies the power of positive influence. You can always choose to make an impact on the lives of others with good, because good you will reap. Even if you do not benefit from doing good to others in the interim, it is a worthwhile investment in the long run. Selfish people lose, but self-less people win. Love your way into people's hearts, and secure for them a destiny superior and memorable. That is how you will secure yours in the end.

The best love you can ever give is unconditional; expecting nothing in return. The ultimate love has been given through Christ's death on the Cross. Yours is to receive it freely and to live it out in full for other human beings. If you don't believe in God, believe at least in this: That no matter how much you think you are worthless, someone above loves you.

The Golden-Platinum Rule

The Golden Rule, or the Law of Love, states that one should do to others what they expect to be done to or for them. The Platinum Rule requires one to ask others how they would like to be treated.

The *Golden-Platinum Rule* goes a step further than both the Golden and the Golden-Platinum principles and requires that what one does to others is what others will do to them, only to them it will come in increased measure; and as much as possible, one should ask others how they would like he or she to treat them.

The Golden-Platinum Rule aspires for a world in which the dignity and humanity of all are above all.

VI

LAWS OF ATTRACTION

16

PRINCIPLES OF ATTRACTION

One of the greatest principles of success
is that if you persist long enough you will
win.
— *Charles Mwewa*

Attracting people to you is actually easier than you think. In the year 2004, I lived in the Alberta's prosperous City of Calgary. I was stunned by the infectious smiles of the Calgarians. Literally, every person whose eyes you met would smile at you. You did not need to be told you were welcome; the smiles were enough. A smile is the basic way of expressing amusement, pleasure, moderate joy, or love, and kindness, by the features of the face. It can be defined as a silent laugh.

Short-Cut to the Heart

The smile opens up people's hearts; it is, as it were, an entrance into people's hearts. Smiles don't lie. You may call them fake, but even by faking a smile you've attempted to open up your heart to someone. A smile brings total wholeness to your body. It is a powerful thing. A smile does for *you* more than it does for other people. But even considering what it does for others, that in itself is enough to make friends and attract other people. To you: smiles banish worry and fatigue; they produce calmness and nourishment to the soul. This is because the source of a true smile is an awakened mind. You relax hundreds of muscles in your face when you smile.

No matter how cold or wintry it is, a smile might be the only sunshine someone sees all day long. So be generous with your smiles. Intuitively, we believe that when someone smiles at us they like us. In fact, when it comes to winning a date, or someone we might later call our wife or husband, a smile is the better indicator. If you smile and she smiles back, you know there is potential to gaining access into her heart.

It is as they say: a smile confuses an approaching frown. And you can be trusted to ensure that there are no smiles available before you put on a frown of any kind. When you get up in the morning, look into the closet of your emotions and choose to put on a smile. With one on you, the world will always look brighter and every curve straighter! Start every day with a smile, and get it over with. It is the most inexpensive way of changing your looks, and the cheapest way of enlisting new friends.

A Way to the Human Soul

Compliments are the keys that open the soul of humans. What you compliment lives; what you criticize dies. Compliment puts premium on contribution and adds value to humanity. Compliment is innovation incognito. It is potential generation and ability activation.

Anyone could be something useful with this tenet. Even a simple compliment like, "You look so good, buddy," can make a difference between potential actualization and gift negligence. Kids are known to be aware of who they could be at a tender age. My daughter, Emmerance, at 18 months old, was able to feel proud when complimented about a new dress. Any enterprise could record a loss without this virtue.

If you've been in the habit of complimenting people, you should understand how powerful compliments are. If you're married you know it is true. Women are not conquered by a complimenting partner, but they will tell you they loath it. They can check themselves in the mirror repeatedly and chuckle, but that is as far as it goes. They do, however, long for that one compliment, "You look good, dear!" and that is enough to win an interview, perform well at work, cook a sumptuous meal, or make your bedroom a paradise of roses!

Likewise, if you tell a guy, "You're the man!" you could get access to a Swiss bank account or even fly to Paris in a private jet! All it takes to open the door to a human soul is a compliment. It's very cheap, but powerful. A compliment is a gesture of hope and appreciation. And that's what we are all doing all day long—trying to win friends, to be understood, appreciated, and recognized for the prowess in who we are.

So why are we not doing what we are one hundred percent certain will bring us the desired results? Perhaps, complimenting is the number-one characteristic of the people we call friendly. They greet us even when we are not prepared for it. They smile at us even when we look grumpy. And they do compliment us even when we feel they are not serious. Compliments make everything feel alright.

At the University of Equal Possibilities

Speaking about the power of a smile and a compliment, there is no culture or language or race where they are not a force to reckon with. I live in Toronto, which perhaps is the most multicultural city in the world. I have worked with people of all backgrounds and cultures. We all may have different skin colors, languages, and names, but two things cause us all to behave in the same way: a smile and a compliment!

As you read this book, you may be hurt, frustrated, or grieving. However grievous your situation is, you can smile your way to wholeness. You can even do more: you can find someone who looks miserable, and pass a compliment. You might be amazed how easy it could be to change someone's gloomy day into a glorious adventure.

In the Opposites

In several parts of the world, in the eighteenth century, people did not have currency. They traded by exchanging goods for goods. In some parts of Africa this trend persisted even as late as the 1980s! People understood that the only means of offsetting their own lack was in trading for those goods and items they didn't have. In return, they had to give away something they had.

The Principle of Opposites is based on the premise that one's lack is compensated for by an opposite, but readily available, aspect. In electronics they say that the north and south poles attract. Magnetism works on an identical principle. There is a way in which we might say that male and female are opposites. And we know that men and women are attracted to each other.

Attention is generated when you present something another does not possess. This principle of exchanges induces interest in people. That sense of presenting something of an opposite nature to others is a powerful force of attraction. People usually ask, "Is there something different?" and by that they mean something of an opposite nature to what they are used to.

You can use the principle of opposites to attract those things or persons in your life that are different from yours. Sometimes you don't need to be like everybody else to influence them; you only need to exert your uniqueness. Most people would agree that they follow a particular philosophy or leader because of its or his uniqueness. To influence people more effectively, you have to discover a particular trait that sets you apart from everyone else. That which makes you different may be the key to your destiny.

There is something like black attracting white. Whether that is between black people and white people, men and women, east and west, or whatever, opposites have a way of living together. My wife is what psychologists might call an introverted phlegmatic personality. I have an extroverted choleric individuality. But we get along pretty well. It is not being opposites, but what you do with them that matters.

Like Attracts Like

Some dating sites like eHarmony.com discovered the mysterious phenomenon of comparing certain traits, temperaments, or emotional, intellectual, social, physical, and other dimensions of compatibility to match couples for successful relationships. All these attempts, thought to be scientifically proven to successfully pair couples, are in fact based on what is commonly referred to as "like attracts like." The concept is not new, although its scientific dimension is adding momentum to the age-old ideal.

The concept of compatibility, or congruence, is a remarkable discovery. But compatibility is not only necessary for couples; it is also necessary for so many areas of life. One of the challenges I have faced in any leadership role I have been privileged to play is the synchronization of different experiences of the participants. One helpful hint is to look for similarities in the ranks, and this turns out to be just the catch.

Just like the principle of opposites, the power of like attracting like is based on individual commitment. Sometimes dealing with an audience which subscribes to similar ideals to those that you hold is an added advantage. It is good for ease of understanding and communication. You don't need to labor too hard to communicate your views, which might be known by your audience anyway.

In political campaigns this works even more effectively. Politicians have used the power of similarities to their advantage. Usually, when a candidate deals with people of a similar orientation, such as culture, background, etcetera, less energy is exerted than is required.

17

RELATIONSHIPS MATTER

When you love people for who they are,
they will show you what they have
— Charles Mwewa

A friend of mine moved from Owen Sound, a small Ontario town, to Toronto, a larger, metropolitan setting and was stunned by the inner-city mentality. In a small town where everybody knew someone, it was easy for him to greet people easily and receive corresponding responses. But in the larger city, everyone seemed to be only interested in their own whims. Attracting people in such settings involves some dexterity.

There is no better way to attract people than by building relationships. It is even more important if you are dealing with voluntary and charitable arrangements. Relationship building is one of the prized ingredients of successful leadership. People will repel you when they, correctly or incorrectly, believe that you are not gregarious. This is because, in human terms, a sociable personality is easier to relate to than an inhibited one. Every leader, regardless of his or her temperament or outlook, must make an effort to build relationships.

Whether people will come back to you is based on how you treat them the first time around. Companies and businesses make it policy to develop courteous relationships with their customers. In fact, especially in telemarketing business lines, you risk being fired more quickly for losing an existing customer than for failing to win a new one. Customer care is not just a good social etiquette; in business, it has become a defining strategy. Organizations spend as much money in customer care-related aspects as in production. This is because they know that a satisfied customer is the one that feels safe with the people he or she is transacting business with.

Relationships build trust. And it is less difficult to win people who trust you than those who doubt you. Some relationships are very important, because they can mean the difference between success and failure. I have noticed that in church environments messaging alone is not enough to keep people. It takes very strong interpersonal relationships to impel the organization ahead. Those members who feel that they are cared for and appreciated usually give more, and are relatively more faithful, than those who may doubt their relationship with their leaders. They say that a bird in the hand is worth two in the bush, and they are right. As a matter of fact, success with your current relationships attracts more in the long run.

People will soon notice if profit is your only motive for craving their attention. One friend (a name I will not disclose) hooked up with me and seemed to be genuinely interested in me. At first, I was so touched by his timely gestures and unceasing desire to communicate. But then I started to notice that he was slowly but surely introducing his real motive for befriending me. It reached a point where he could hide no more, and he began to pester me into making certain donations.

Another man started in a similar way, but later I discovered that his reason for getting close was so that I could invite him to speak to our group. I don't dispute the idea of speaking engagements, since even I do get frequent invitations to speak to different groups. But what I was obstinate about was the motive. If friendships were based on certain favors, what would happen when those favors were lived out?

When you begin to think about the extremes to which advertising companies and even individuals are reaching in trying to woo people's attention, you might begin to doubt whether in the future people will be valued for who they are. As it stands, if someone suddenly becomes too close and very loving to you, you begin to suspect something fishy. Usually you will discover in the next few days the real motive for such gestures.

Being genuinely interested in people pays. There are three things you need to do to truly become interested in people. First, get close to someone with the intention to understand and help. The test of friendship character is whether someone you call a friend is willing to go the extra mile for you without asking for something in turn. Society is trying to tell us every single day through the media that we cannot help each other unless we benefit from such help. Charity shouldn't be paired with merit.

Second, understand that friendship is a human need, not a calculated want. Therein lies the difference: needs are things we can't do without, while wants are things we *can* do without. Friendship is a human necessity. People are doing you a favor by befriending you. Without genuine friends, your life is empty and lonely. Friends brighten up your day and offer you a reason to be truly happy.

Third, allow other people to come first, before yourself. Can you do that? Can you put your colleagues, friends, relatives, or family and their interests before yourself? If you can do that, you can show that you are genuinely interested in people. The Bemba people of Northern Zambia have a saying that parental care is an investment into the future. What that simply means is that when people perceive that you are genuinely interested in them they will reciprocate in deed or in kind. When you love people for who they are, they will show you what they have.

18

LEVELS OF ATTRACTION

All things being equal, dress to suite the occasion, and speak to exceed people's expectations.
— Charles Mwewa

There are three major levels of attraction when it comes to influencing people: you can think it at the mental level, or you can show it at the physical level. You can also say it. Basically, to be understood, or heard, you've got to intelligently say what you want. Saying what you want is a subject of social persuasion which we discussed at length in Part Two. Here we shall discuss the other two, specifically, how you can attract people through positive thinking and dressing. We shall begin with the later. Wardrobe, as they call it, is one of the ways in which you make statements. If you met two people on the street, how would you tell the difference? How would you know which one worked in an office and which one didn't, for example?

You Are What You Wear

What we wear defines who we are. The television show, *You're What You Wear* could not be far from the truth! People can immediately be attracted to you, or reject you, based on what you wear. I am a public speaker and I see the importance of dressing for the occasion. Intuitively, the audience will take roughly the same time it takes you to adjust to stage fright, to evaluate your dress code. When it is satisfied, mentally, about not just what you are wearing but also about its quality, then it will be ready to listen to you. All things being equal, dress to suite the occasion, and speak to exceed people's expectations. Dressing tells a lot about your behavior and comportment.

If you are going to leave a lasting impact in people's lives and attract them to you, you cannot be careless about your dressing habits. You must follow trends in vogue and know which styles are in fashion. In North America this means understanding the impact of the seasons on dressing. Do you understand what brand-name power means? It pays to wear a Nike or Adidas—

do you know that? You can be personally very comfortable about what you wear, but society puts certain premiums on different aspects of attire. When you ignore what you wear, people will ignore what you say, that's for sure. Make it a rule to always dress to attract.

There is a difference between being modesty and over-illustrious. Spend within your means but aim for quality. We don't have to spend a year's salary on a single outfit if we want to look stylish. Experts in fashion advise us to buy one or two pieces of high-quality clothing that we will dry clean and fuss over. This garment should last us for years. Rule of the thumb is to mix and match our high-quality garment with inexpensive, washable clothing that we may replace every couple of seasons.

Clarice, my partner, has a hold on fashion and style. In fact, she may not end a week without reference to a particular garment she saw in a store somewhere. But what I like most about her, when it comes to buying clothes, is that she least spends outside her means and yet she looks truly great. What is her secret? My observation is that she follows the approach I have referred to above. She invests in few exquisite, showcase pieces of clothing. Then she mixes and matches them with other inexpensive attires. This truly lends style and class to anything else she wears.

A leader cannot be careless when it comes to dressing. Leadership is influence, and by dressing appropriately you are making a strong statement to the people you lead. Your dress *ethos* will give you an upper hand when it comes to perception. The way people perceive you may determine how they will react to you or your message.

The Law of Attraction

The Law of Attraction is commonly associated with New Thought theories. It states that people experience the corresponding manifestations of their predominant thoughts, feelings, words, and actions, and that people therefore have direct control over reality and their lives through thought alone. A person's thoughts, emotions, beliefs, and actions are said to attract corresponding positive and negative energies. The law of attraction states literally that you get what you think about, and your thoughts determine your destiny.

Many proponents of the idea claim that, with practice, people can use the law of attraction to change their lives. My interest in the Law of Attraction is in the way it can help people to tap into their inner power to positively influence society. Our actions and words attract positive or negative experiences. In relationships, what you do and say, and how you do so to others, is very important.

As a Man Thinks

People become what they think, and eventually *do* according to what they have thought. Therefore, our thoughts attract like energy when introduced into reality. Many critics rebuff this belief, but what they forget is that the idea is not new. It is not a "new age" ideology, as they claim. In fact, in the Hebrew scripture of Proverbs 23:7, it has long been stated that: "As a man thinks in his heart, so is he."

A person *is* his or her thought if mental disorders do not interfere. When you think about positive things you attract positive outcomes. It is like the concept of *Garbage in-garbage out* in computer programming. People who have made a difference in the lives of others believed they could. You can equally change things around you through positive thinking.

People everywhere are discovering the power of positive thinking. In March 2006, a film called *The Secret* was developed around the Law of Attraction and was later developed into a book by the same title. The movie and book sold at an extraordinary pace and gained widespread attention across the media. Why the hustle? Is it because people are discovering that thoughts have an energy that attracts like energy?

There are few things that I believe can translate this energy into something tangible. The first one is the power of prayer. We now know that God is the source of creative energy. By knowing our desires and asking him about them, we allow this creative energy to recreate similar results in our lives.

Haven't you been amazed that something you had only had strong thoughts about actually came to pass? Most people tell me that they desired this particular thing and thought so much about it, sort of making a silent prayer, and bang! It turned out to be. What happened? Was it mere coincidence or sheer luck? I don't think so. These people attracted a similar energy to create what they had desired, and unconsciously asked for.

Secondly, develop a strong mental picture about what you want to attract. This is called envisioning. It involves focusing your thoughts upon the desired thing with enormous zest. The creative power is able to do far more than you can believe or imagine. But wait a minute—notice here: it is about imaginations, isn't it? Positively so! There is a creative mental process in all of us. It begins with a strong desire. That desire then leads to envisioning, which is the same thing as imagining. Imagination leads to believing. Finally, it becomes the manifestation of what you desired.

Thirdly, and finally, the manifestation of the desired outcome ensues in two stages. Stage one is called the positioning phase. This is when you feel and behave just like you would if the outcome was already on its way. It is having the substance of the things hoped for, and behaving as though you have the evidence of the unseen reality. Calling those things that are not as if they were, is a profound precursor to the manifested reality.

Stage two is the actualization phase, where you become open to receiving. For the most part, most people know how to ask or even how to imagine the outcome. In the following section we shall discuss how you can receive what you ask for or imagine. I call this the Law of Importunity.

The Law of Importunity

Receiving could be both passive and active. Passive reception is when you believe it is not in your power to know how what you desire would manifest. So you rest, knowing that by some means your dreams will come to pass someday. Your role here is simply to have a strong desire and hope that you have sufficiently tapped into the unseen energy. This is what you could refer to as the quintessential law of positive thinking.

There is a dimension of attraction that I believe rules the business-minded world. It is what I call the Law of Importunity. It is adding a degree of persistence to receiving. When you ask, you will receive. But sometimes just asking is not enough; some kind of persistence is needed. This could manifest itself into seeking for the things you desire and even searching for them.

How does the marketing industry gain access to our most treasured dollar? Or how do we end up accepting services and goods which we never wanted in the first place? By persisting with the demand for our attention, and by appealing to our sense of greed, the marketing industry has wooed us into succumbing to its demands.

On the positive side, you can make use of this law to attract people to the better side. Lobbyists can bring massive awareness to needy areas or issues that need serious attention, by persisting in their quest. Ministers of religion, human rights advocates, charities, etcetera, can rely on this law to stir society into making better laws and choices for the good of the world.

The law of importunity is a needed weapon to achieve particular goals and aspirations. This law insists on persisting, with a kind of never-giving-up mentality. Persistence attracts success. Even when everything seems to be blurred, keep your head above the water. Nelson Mandela never gave up on the hope that the apartheid regime would crumble one day in

South Africa. In 1994 Nelson Mandela went on to become the first black president of South Africa. The secret: he never gave up. His resolute persistence attracted a celebrated victory.

19

IN THE BOOKS

Reading builds the spirit within us,
breaks through intellectual barriers, and
gives us a platonic invincibility.
— Charles Mwewa

A critical mark of influencers is that they are sticklers to study. They read critical books [and eBooks], and energize their minds. Show me a man who reads, and I will show you a creative mind. How grateful we should all be to God for books! Put books in the hands of intelligent minds, and they breed geniuses. Give a thinker a book, and he becomes an inventor. There is no limit to what books can do. A boy in a village somewhere can break through the labyrinth of ignorance and illiteracy, and wear an aristocratic mind, through books.

Ben Carson in *Think Big* gives us three benefits of reading books. First of all, reading books gives you the power to enlarge yourself by broadening your knowledge and information base. As a man thinks, so he is. If your thinking is narrow, so will be your world. The fact is, you can't rise higher than you think. Your life is a definition of what you know and think. There is no better way to enlarge your world than through reading books.

Within books are the thoughts and wisdom of past minds and experiences. When we read, we interact with these minds. In essence, these minds continue to talk to us and to provide us with significant insights. They give us the perspectives we never knew about life and things. They elevate us to their levels, so that we begin to think like them or better. Reading books builds the spirit within us, breaks through intellectual barriers, and gives us a platonic invincibility.

At the writing of this book my second-born daughter, Tashany-Idyllia, was just weeks over two years old. I had observed with religious intensity each stage in her development. I was flabbergasted with the intricacy of her small brain. I was convinced beyond doubt that babies are born with creative ability. Children are born with innate ability to respond to stimuli and to meet the needs around them. They use imagination to come up with innovative ideas.

Most importantly, babies can use these imaginations to find new ways to react to new situations. It is amazing how they get your attention to change their diapers, give them food, and perform various theatrics. Psychologists believe that we lose this creativity as we grow older. We need a secondary source to refill this pure creativity. And the nearest resource is books. Books not only increase our knowledge, but also create for us infinite improvement possibilities.

Second, reading books stretches our existence in more ways than one. It challenges our exclusiveness and makes us nimble. Reading makes us leaders because we begin to see what others are not seeing. And leaders must be readers, because they have to expand their worldview so as to lead people competently.

Third, reading books opens doors to significance. There is a farcical saying that if you want to hide anything from a black man, put it in a book. Of course, the adage holds no water. But what is true to all, black or white, is that reading makes your life full, significant, and interesting.

Success is not a monopoly of certain temperaments or personality traits. It is a concoction of many ideas gone before. Through books, we learn how to tap into the ideas of many noble and brilliant brains. We gain insights into how others have triumphed over similar circumstances. Reading books turns our limited dreams into limitless possibilities. Reading books is a symbol of influence. You cannot be a reader and be nothing in life. Reading books does something to you—it refuses to let you fail, even if you choose to. Books will take you somewhere in life; read them.

VII

THE LAW OF ENVISIONING

20

THE LAW OF VISION

People perish due to lack of vision
—Proverbs 21:18

Most scholars define a vision as a mental picture of a future state. Some see it as a blueprint, or a master plan of a proposed undertaking. The beauty about a vision is that you don't need to define it right to benefit from it. In fact, most people who have accomplished greatly didn't even know that they had a vision. They might have called it a strong desire, a dream, a burden, or anything else. But whatever they called it, they had one thing in common: it was what these people felt they would be very happy to do. It inspired confidence within them and motivated them to sacrifice all to achieve it.

I remember in 2001 I attended a meeting which was dubbed Strategic Planning and Visioning. At this meeting, the moderator labored very hard to define a vision and to differentiate it from strategic objectives. Although this was not my first time listening to a discourse on vision, I can confess I came out of that meeting more confused than anything else. Most people who lecture on vision simply repeat what they have read; they are not visionaries themselves. When you observe visionaries, you see one constant thing about them: they are submerged in the vision. Everything they say or do is suffused by that vision. A visionary and his vision are one and the same thing.

I am a visionary. Everywhere I go I always begin something from the scratch. I derive so much joy in seeing an idea take root and become a reality. And any visionary will tell you that it is more difficult to dream a life changing dream than to inherit one already began by someone else. Literally everything I began exists even to date.

From Point A to B

In fact, vision is very common to all of us. When moving from point A to point B, we all have a vision of some sort. It begins with what I call a panoramic vision. Panoramic vision is the physical disposition we take towards the desired destination. Thus, if we want to go to the East, we may first look up and view the East before we embark on the journey. This act gives us a general feeling about the destination.

The Point of Excitement

The panoramic vision is the excitement stage of visioning. Everyone who ever dreamed came to a stage when they saw the vision as good as done. They were so imbued into it that they were filled with excitement. This stage enables the visionary to begin making movements, to be restless, as it were.

When I was beginning the *World Influence Vision (WIV)*, I was so excited that I rarely spent a minute without being aware of it. I talked about it to everyone and repeated it incessantly. I saw it in everything I watched, and heard about it from anywhere I listened. I was constantly *seeing* what others were not seeing. I talked about it in the present simply because I was very excited about the idea. Fifteen years after the fact, *WIV* stands strong, producing influential books and creative materials able to, indeed, influence the world.

By the Big Brown Tree

The Bemba tribe is the largest in Zambia. In the olden times, before the advent of a modern system of transportation, as in most tribes in Africa, people relied on the word of mouth for direction and transmission of information. So, when you reached a particular village and asked about the route to your destination, you were told that it was just by the big, brown tree. Nobody had ever seen the big, brown tree. But the idea of the tree being nearby gave the traveler the impression that he or she was nearing the destination. Rather than becoming frustrated, travelers were revitalized to continue the journey.

That's how the vision works. It gives the person a sense of excitement, even though the undertaking itself is overwhelming. Most visionaries legitimately know visions are impossible enterprises. But they also genuinely believe that the vision will materialize. How is this possible? Excitement! They are so excited and motivated that the likelihood of failure never bothers them at all. They see, as it were, the reality of their dreams by the big, brown tree!

From Panoramic to Conceptual Visioning

The excitement stage naturally leads to the reality stage when the visionary begins to come to grips with the practicality of the vision. In order to bring the vision to reality, the visionary goes through what we may refer to as mental conception. At this stage, many would call a vision a mental picture. It is a mental picture of what could be. Naturally, here the vision will begin to be broken down into workable facets.

At the panoramic phase the vision was only "to influence the world." From the general vision at the panoramic phase, the vision then comes to a much more specific conceptual stage and becomes "to influence the world through books," for example. The vision may still be written down as influencing the world, but conceptually speaking, the visionary understands it fully as influencing the world through books.

It would be very hard to make most visions materialize without the help of other people. When you conceive a vision, it is wisest to accumulate a group of people who must share in the vision. Understandably, this is the most important stage in the life of any vision. However smart or experienced the visionary may be, bringing the vision to pass is a team responsibility. If you want to be a good boxer or a great soccer player, you will require not only a good coach, but you must also be a good team player.

We all praise the guy who dreamed, but we fail to acknowledge the people who help make the vision a reality. These people are as important as the person who began the vision, because without them the vision would most likely not materialize. The visionary must carefully select a group of people who must share in the vision. These people become a conduit through which the vision is both augmented and spread.

From Conceptual to Experiential Visioning

Communicating the vision is very necessary to what I call the Experiential Vision. Vision has the power in itself to produce actions that are necessary for the fulfillment of the vision. The trouble with all of us is that we hope for the vision to work immediately. The vision may not work out immediately even if it has been well communicated. Persistence and the ability to endure are needed in the fulfillment of a vision.

It is believed that if you're determined enough you can reach over half of your goals, and more. Life is full of surprises. One of these surprises is that sometimes the race is not won by the swift, or the battle by the strong, or riches possessed by people with great understanding, or favor by the people with skill. There is, however, one thing to the advantage of all of us: persistent determination.

There is nothing in this world that can take the place of persistent determination in your quest to fulfill your vision. Talent, ability, genius or education may, especially, not, but persistent determination alone is matchless.

Determination produces hope, which is essential in the fulfillment of the vision. Because life is full of ups and downs, living without hope is dangerous. There is usually no guarantee that your situation will improve on its own without external influence. People cannot be trusted because they change without warning. Hope conquers all fears. The capacity for hope is the most significant fact of life. It provides human beings with a sense of destination and the energy to get started. A hopeful person believes in his or her efforts. The power of hope is that it serves you under difficult situations. It is believed that people who are hopeful are better able to bear up under trying circumstances.

Usually on the road to fulfilling our visions there will be ups and downs. The worst of these gulping downs is disappointment. Disappointments are common in our world. Every one of us will be disappointed at one time or the other. The problem with disappointments is that no one is equipped to endure them. When they attack, they are unbearable. But knowledge will save us. Knowledge that disappointments are only temporary setbacks, and not permanent landmarks, will sustain us in distressing times.

End in Mind

So you have a dream—press on. You're losing your bearing—stay on course and hope. If you've been disappointed, understand that there are more appointments in your future. All these translate into determination, and your destiny waits! Vision gives you the power to enjoy the joys of the future today. Can you imagine being excited about what has not happened yet? Can you imagine living as if you have already arrived? That's what vision does to you. It enables you to live.

Without a vision, without a mental picture of an eminent future, people perish. People who have something to live for have a greater chance to survive the storms of life. Those who have nothing to live for expire before their time. Do you want to live longer and see better days?

Live with a vision. The vision will keep you active, alert, and healthy. Vision drives you. It is the end you have in mind. The man, who can drive himself further, once the effort gets painful, is the man who will achieve something in life. Stick your neck out and press ahead. What will differentiate an unsuccessful from a successful person is not a lack of strength or knowledge, but a lack of vision.

By Vision I Wrote This Book

When you lose wealth, you have lost much. When you lose a friend, you have lost more. But when you live without a vision, you have nothing. What is your vision of your family, career, or profession? What do you want to be remembered for? I wrote this book with vision. I believe that the book will enable you to live with a mission and leave a mark on life. The future belongs to those who are willing to make short-term sacrifices for long-term gains.

The difference between leaders and followers is in the way they view the future. Leaders envision a future filled with possibilities, while followers wait to be told what is good for them. If you want to graduate from being a follower to being a leader, you must learn to listen to your heart. You must believe in the impossible and hope in the incredible. Leaders live with vision. They see with their hearts. When you work with your whole heart, you will succeed.

EPILOGUE

What is happiness? What truly makes people happy? These two questions have covered more territory than any other in human history. We are reaching far and wild in search of the true meaning of happiness. The paradox of the matter is that even those who seem to have found it still look for more. It gives the impression that there will be no end to the pursuit of happiness. One would have thought that, given the technological advancements, the scientific explosions, the communication spurts, and talismanic economy of most of the developed world, a reasonable sense of stability would have been found. Yet, day and night, people are restless; those who have want even more, and those who do not have believe there is something more for them.

Here is a simple truth about life; it is short and limited. Immediately we are born, we begin to die. The more we acquire on earth, the more sorrowful we become. And the paradox is that a fool or a naïve and lazy relative will make use of all our labor and diligence. The more money we have, the more we should give it out.

When you give out happiness, you receive happiness. The more you withhold it to yourself, the more miserable you get. True happiness is achieved through small things like giving, sharing, loving and friendship, not in winning a lottery.

There is no plagiarism with ideas about happiness; everybody is happy. If an author's works make others happy, he or she has also achieved happiness.

A Prescription for Happiness

Here is one thing that is true: those who will be really happy are those who will have sought and found how to serve. Most people erroneously believe that greatness is in being served. True greatness, however, consists of giving and serving others. Half of the world is on the wrong scent in the pursuit of happiness. They think it consists of having and getting, and in being served by others. As they progress in life, they begin to discover that that is a fluke. But if one dearly wants to be truly happy, he or she has to seek not to be served, but to serve, and to give of him or herself to the service of another.

Jesus upset the *modus operandi* of leadership when he insists that a great leader is the one who washes his or her servants' feet. For he understands that true greatness lies in stooping down for those you lead. Serving others here does not mean the instituted protocol or obeying the rules of social etiquette in deliberating public and official affairs. Superiors, as a matter of fact, deserve to be treated to some form of respect. What is meant, however, is the unselfish attitude of being selflessly given to the service and well-being of others, regardless of social standing.

The person who lives for himself or herself is a failure; the person who lives for others has achieved true success and happiness. The world we live in is increasingly becoming self-centered. We heap the most accolades on the ingenious, the shrewd, and the ruthless. We praise masculinity and honor guile. We think that to be compassionate and loving is a weakness. We sacrifice personal tranquility for personal glory. We pursue the appearance of happiness with everything we have, disregarding the immortal virtues of trustworthiness, righteousness, fairness, equity, kindness, and care. Yet the real measure of a person's legacy is not how much he or she held in bank accounts, *but what he or she did with it to better another human's life.* When you live a life full of compassion, you have fulfilled all morality.

Real service is an effort to make someone else happy. Happiness is not the end product. Happiness is a by-product of an attempt to make another person happy. Most people go all out in the pursuit of happiness, and are frustrated and disgruntled when they fail to find it. You cannot look for happiness without changing something about yourself. Countless millions of people are busy chasing after money, popularity, fame, and power, believing that such acquisitions will bring them happiness.

Riches without charity are worth nothing. *They are a blessing only to the one who makes them a blessing to others.* And that is what leads to happy existence. It is not through being rich, or famous, or popular, or powerful that you attain happiness—while these are important, they are not enough. It is in doing something worthwhile with your riches, fame or power, for another human being, that true happiness is found. Do something, even if it is small, to make others happier and better, because that is the highest ambition, the most elevating hope, which can inspire a human being.

The paradox of happiness is that it is not always found in straight boulevards and paved avenues. Sometimes happiness is embedded in trouble, misfortunes, paid, and adverse circumstances. When you think about happiness, think of the gold-refinery process. The finest of gold comes out, but from higher refinery temperatures.

Most happiness is found in your troubled experiences. If you will call your troubles experiences, and remember that every experience develops some latent force within you, you will grow vigorous and happy. Do not let your negative circumstances and adverse experiences rob you of your happiness. A person who is happy is the one who refuses to be pounded into the mortar of misfortune; he or she sees instead an opportunity in every adversity.

Conclusion of the Matter

When all has been said and done, remember that honesty will win you the day and fairness will create for you the way. Kindness will secure for you the bay, good will save you from the sway and charity will increase your pay. It is a mark of true happiness to find inspiration in those things and activities that make other people better in the end.

ABOUT THE AUTHOR

CHARLES MWEWA

Charles Mwewa is a Dad, a husband, a prolific author and researcher, poet, novelist, political thinker, a law instructor, and Christian and community leader. Mwewa has written no less than 30 books and counting. Mwewa, his wife and their three daughters, reside in the Canadian Capital City of Ottawa.

AUTHOR'S CONTACT

Email address:

spynovel2016@gmail.com

Facebook:

www.facebook.com/charlesmwewa

Twitter:

https://twitter.com/BooksMwewa

Instagram:

instagram.com/mwewabooks/?hl=en

Author's website:

https://www.charlesmwewa.com

To order this book online:

https://www.amazon.com/dp/1988251532

INDEX

F

G

73, 75, 76, 87, 97,
99, 101, 102, 108,
121, 122, 124, 129,
136, 140, 143, 156,
167, 174, 180, 189,
202, 203, 212, 219,
221
influencer, 5, 43
influencers, 42, 209
infomercials, 65
information, 21, 137,
154, 209, 218
inspiration, 3, 23, 24,
51, 111, 229
instructions, 16
integrity, 6, 102, 167,
169, 170, 171, 172,
173, 174, 175
intelligent minds, 209
Internet, 66, 67, 166
intimidation, 53
intolerance, 5, 105
investment, 13, 180,
197
investments, 120
Iraq, 42
Irene, 14, 26
Italian Serie A, 118

J

Jacob, 60
Jesus, 66, 93, 151, 153,
226
Jew, 17
job, 7, 18, 33, 35, 42,
52, 55, 56, 97, 117,
126, 136, 142, 146
John Edwards, 43
John Q, 83
Joseph, 14
joy, 14, 18, 20, 62, 107,
108, 111, 138, 183,
216
judgments, 34
Julius Caesar, 41
justice, 39, 88

K

Kardashians, 178
Kayi Tribe, 24
Kind Law of Caring,
79
kindness, 83, 84, 90,
100, 139, 183, 227
Kitchener, 146
knockout, 98
Kofi Annan, 77

L

longevity, 43

lottery, 88, 114, 226

love, 6, 7, 14, 18, 20,
25, 49, 55, 59, 79,
82, 94, 95, 104, 112,
120, 135, 136, 138,
139, 140, 141, 142,
143, 166, 177, 180,
183, 193, 197

LSAT, 154

M

Mado, 14

Magna International
Inc., 146

Mahatma Gandhi, 77

Major Soccer League,
118

manipulate, 3

Marcus Brutus, 41

Mark Antony, 41, 42

Martin Luther King,
Jr., 77

materialism, 23

mathematician, 162

mathematics, 154

media, 25, 96, 118,
165, 196, 204

mental picture, 132,

205, 215, 219, 222

millionaires, 89

mistake, 53, 109, 114,
115, 116

Mohammed Ali, 119

money, 12, 13, 14, 42,
44, 57, 85, 88, 114,
121, 125, 139, 146,
150, 194, 225, 228

monopoly, 212

moral agreement, 170

moral disagreement,
171

Mother Theresas, 96

motivator, 69

motive, 55, 59, 136,
141, 195, 196

mutiny, 41, 42

N

nation, 2, 7, 42, 43, 95,
140, 156

negligence, 25, 103,
185

neighbor, 92, 177, 178

network, 108

never-giving-up
mentality, 207

O

obedience, 71, 72
observation, 35, 201
Ole la Liga, 118
Ontario, xiv, 63, 84, 193
opinions, 28, 33, 49, 52
opportunity, 2, 60, 65, 73, 85, 100, 108, 110, 120, 128, 229
oratory, 38
Orbit Principle, 179
orphans, 86
Oscar De La Hoya, 118
ovation, 75

P

panoramic vision, 216
paralegals, 17, 43
parent, 140
past glory, 118, 119
pathos, 45
persistence, 206, 208
personal comfort, 16
persuasion, 3, 4, 31, 33, 34, 37, 38, 40, 42, 43, 45, 47, 56,

57, 59, 75, 76, 77, 199
philanthropic, 139
philanthropists, 15
philosophy, 31, 55, 189
phobias, 113
pioneers, 15
Plato, 38, 77
point A, 125, 216
point B, 125, 216
policy, 37, 38, 40, 41, 45, 55, 123, 194
politicians, 42, 146
politics, 165
popularity, 12, 58, 228
position, 13, 43, 45, 52, 56, 94, 117, 119, 139, 143
positive thinking, 199, 204, 206
posterity, 102
poverty, 19, 86
power, 2, 6, 12, 18, 23, 24, 25, 31, 40, 43, 45, 55, 59, 62, 90, 91, 95, 102, 118, 119, 122, 124, 136, 147, 148, 155, 159, 167, 180, 187, 190, 191, 200, 203, 204,